SIGNS OF LIFE

20 Catholic Customs

and Their Biblical Roots

SCOTT HAHN

An abridged version of
Signs of Life: 40 Catholic Customs
and Their Biblical Roots

IMAGE

To Veronica Margaret Hahn,
my first grandchild

IMAGE

Nihil Obstat: Monsignor Michael F. Hull, STD, Censor Librorum.
Imprimatur: Most Reverend Dennis J. Sullivan, Auxiliary Bishop and Vicar General,
Archdiocese of New York

The *Nihil Obstat* and *Imprimatur* are official declarations that a book or pamphlet
is free of doctrinal or moral error. No implication is contained therein that those
who have granted the *Nihil Obstat* or *Imprimatur* agree with the content, opinions, or
statements expressed.

Published in the United States by Image, an imprint of the Crown Publishing Group,
a division of Penguin Random House LLC, New York. Originally published in the
United States in hardcover and in significantly different form as SIGNS OF LIFE:
40 CATHOLIC CUSTOMS AND THEIR BIBLICAL ROOTS by Image,
an imprint of the Crown Publishing Group, a division of
Penguin Random House LLC, New York in 2009.

ImageCatholicBooks.com

IMAGE is a registered trademark and the "I" colophon is a
trademark of Penguin Random House LLC.

Library of Congress Cataloging-in-Publication Data
Hahn, Scott.
Signs of Life : 40 Catholic Customs and Their
Biblical Roots / by Scott Hahn. — 1st ed.
p. cm.
I. Catholic Church—Doctrines. 2. Catholic Church—
Customs and practices. I. Title.
BX1754.H16 2009
282—dc22 2009012276

ISBN: 978-0-385-51949-6
Augustine Exclusive ISBN: 9780525615835

2018 Augustine Institute Exclusive Edition

Contents

IV *Spice of Life*

V *Abundant Life*

VI *Love of My Life*

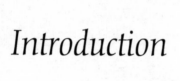

Introduction

Signs of Life

No matter what line of work we're in, no matter the circumstances of our personal life, we all come to days when we face a wall—a wall too sheer to climb, too high to vault, too strong to topple. These walls can arise, for instance, as problems on the job or in relationships. We try everything humanly possible to get over, around, under, or through them. But we reach a point where there's nothing left to try.

I've faced many of those moments, and one I recall vividly. I was a young scholar, with a young family. I was working on my doctoral thesis, the crowning work of my studies in theology, and I came upon a problem in the interpretation of a certain verse of the Bible. It was a small passage, but it was a big problem, and the verse itself was a key to my argument. So I had to work out all the interpretive kinks before I could defend my thesis before the interrogators on my doctoral committee. In fact, *unless* I worked out the kinks, I was almost sure to fail.

I read all the available commentaries and found nothing useful—not a single glimmer of light, except the sympathy of scholars who had faced the same wall before I did. I dithered and puttered and pondered and paced—for months—but I couldn't find a way forward. This was a real problem, as I had already invested several years in my research. If I abandoned the project now, I faced a long, hard, and humiliating trek back to the beginning of the thesis-approval process.

Then the wall got even higher.

My adviser, a Jesuit priest, called to inform me that he had been transferred to Rome, Italy, to the Gregorian University. I had to complete my dissertation immediately, he said, or search out a new adviser, who might or might not find my thesis plausible.

I stopped sleeping and intensified my efforts, poring over tomes and making late-night calls to scholars I had never met.

Nothing. The wall loomed higher now than ever. On the far side of the wall stretched a professorial career . . . the possibility of tenure . . . open doors for honors, jobs, and publications. On this side, at least as I saw it: professional ruin.

I put myself through several weeks of this when something truly remarkable happened. My adviser called again. He just wanted to make sure I was prepared for *anything* that could happen when I showed up to defend my thesis. And so he went through a list of potential difficulties and obstacles I had not considered before, but that I should expect to encounter on the big day.

I recognized defeat. But I could not admit it. I was too proud. Yet I recognized that, too, as a problem. On top of all that, I was sleep deprived and overcaffeinated, which made my mind a tangle of moral and academic problems of biblical proportions.

There was nothing left for me to do. So I had to do *something*.

CROSS PURPOSES

I had been Roman Catholic only a short while by the time of this crisis—a little less than a decade—but my memory and imagination were already stuffed full of incidents from the lives of the saints, as any ten-year-old's should be.

Please don't get me wrong. I'm not saying I'm a Francis of Assisi or Ignatius Loyola. Nor am I trying to turn up the melodrama. In the great sweep of history, my thesis mattered little. In my professional life, however, it was make or break. The biographies of the saints, I've learned over the years, are made to serve as models for precisely this sort of crisis.

The wall was very high. Yet, very late one night, and quite suddenly, I knew of something much higher than that wall, and I knew what I must do. I put on my jacket and set off into the night, not even bothering to comb my hair.

The neighborhood streets were still and dark. The quickest way to the campus where I teach is straight up the street and through the woods, so that's the way I went.

My goal—the thing so much higher than my wall—was always before me on the horizon. Towering above the dorms and library and labs of Franciscan University of Steubenville is a sixty-foot steel cross, illuminated and visible from the interstate highways, and even from across the Ohio River in West Virginia.

I made my way hastily across the silent campus. If anyone had seen me, they would surely have concluded that too much studying had made me crazy (see Acts 26:24). My mind was surely vexed, but probably as sound as it had ever been, as I found myself at the foot of that shining, colossal cross.

There I didn't have to think hard. I knew what the saints of history had done. I needed to do something. I needed to do what they did.

I kissed the cross, and then I lay flat, face down at the foot of the cross, and I cried.

By then I had filled myself up with all the best the world had to offer. I had consulted the most respected research libraries and personally called upon the top rank of scholars. None of that was enough. And I told that to Jesus: my wall was far too high. Yet I knew, no matter what I was going through, his cross was still higher.

For he had at his disposal a lot more than I had. Nevertheless, even *though he was God*, "he did not count equality with God a thing to be grasped, but emptied himself, taking the form of a servant, being born in the likeness of men. And being found in human form he humbled himself and became obedient unto death, even death on a cross" (Phil 2:6–8).

Lying there with my face in the dirt, I gave him everything, in the way I knew from St. Francis and countless others. I told him that if I had to fail, so be it: I would be emptied as he was.

Here's Mud in Your Eye

What happened next?

I'll get to that in a few minutes. First I'd like to stop and consider the beauty of the Catholic life.

Sometimes we find that we've arrived at a wall. Sometimes we find that we've just hit the wall, at high speed—and we've left our crash helmet at home. When that happens, something in our nature cries out to us: *Don't just stand there. Do something!* God created us that way. He created us with bodies built for action, and he set us to work in a world full of things to do.

All through history, he has acknowledged this natural tendency and given us things to do. When the people were thirsty, God instructed Moses to strike a rock so that water would gush forth. Why did he do that? Not because he needed to. He could have dropped canteens from the clouds, or installed a great lake in the midst of the desert, or even had angels serve up pitchers of margaritas. Yet he knew human nature, and he knew our need to *do something*. So he gave Moses something to do.

From the time of Moses to the time of Jesus, nothing about human nature had changed. Jesus could have cured the blind with a simple nod or a word, but he didn't. He made a paste of mud and spit, and then he sent the blind man off to wash in a nearby pond.

Still another time, Jesus made the healing of lepers contingent on their going to show themselves to the Temple priests. "And as they went they were cleansed" (Lk 17:14).

The Catholic life—the great Christian tradition—is a tremendous inheritance from two millennia of saints in many lands and circumstances. Being Catholic means never having to say we have nothing left to do. Our prayer is enriched by sacred images and incense, votive candles and rosary beads, waters and oils, gestures and postures, blessings and medals, customs and ceremonies.

Because I was learning to live a Catholic life, I was able to say that even alone at three o'clock in the morning in my study, even in the midst of a professional crisis—even when there was nothing more to do—I could do something.

I could leave immediately and make a pilgrimage.
I could prostrate myself in prayer.
I could venerate the holy cross.
I could invoke the Scriptures.

In fact, I could do all these things, and no one was awake to stop me. So I did.

Putting Things in Order

The Catholic life is full of such things. Yet we don't always understand why they're in our tradition. Even devout Catholics can treat these many and diverse customs as if they're disconnected and random acts—superstitions that have somehow gained the Church's approval.

For this reason, you'll sometimes hear Catholic intellectuals sneer at popular piety. That's the last thing I want to do, first of all because Jesus had greater praise for simple believers and children than he had for the intellectuals of his day, and I assume the same rules of human nature still apply. Second of all, because I know that Catholic popular devotions are indeed well-grounded in Scripture—as I hope to show in the course of this book—and that they were practiced by the leading lights of the Catholic intellectual tradition. Finally, because I know many people who are holier than I am but have had no opportunities for theological education. In fact, many canonized saints had no formal education whatsoever. So intellectuals would do well to pray their beads along with the pious sodalities in the parish. It beats sneering any day of the week. Louis Pasteur was one of the intellectual giants of the modern age; yet he prayed his Rosary like a child.

What's more, it's a mistake to treat *intelligence* and *piety* as if they're mutually exclusive terms. The best thing we can do is to offer our devotions with understanding. Jesus instructed us not to pray like theologians who are hypocrites (Mt 6:5); but neither does he want us to pray like pagans who don't have a clue what they're doing (Mt 6:7). A saint of the twentieth century, St. Josemaría Escrivá, put the matter very well. He urged Catholics to have both the wisdom of theologians and the piety of children.

As Catholics, we are free to cultivate a rich life of piety, drawing from the treasures of many lands and many ages. "But," as St. Paul said, "all things should be done decently and in order" (I Cor 14:40).

This book, then, is a celebration of all things Catholic, and the biblical doctrine that makes them Catholic. But it's more than that. It's a handbook, a how-to, a good-natured defense, and a gentle nudge for all of us to do better, no matter where we are in our spiritual development.

One of my goals in writing this book is to show how Catholic customs and devotions fit into the larger scheme of Christian faith. Our first order of business is to develop a new way of seeing, a new way of growing in wisdom and knowledge. That way is traditionally called *mystagogy*.

READING THE SIGNS

The English word *mystagogy* comes from the Greek *mystagogia*, which means "guidance in the mysteries." In the mystagogical instruction of the early Church, a clergyman (usually the local bishop) would take the time to explain the small details of the liturgy and how they corresponded symbolically to the events that played out in the Bible. This method reaches back to the New Testament itself, where St. Paul and St. Peter spoke of baptism and Eucharist as the fulfillment of Old Testament foreshadowings (see, for example, I Cor 10:2–17; I Pet 3:18–21).

Mystagogy enables new believers to see beyond the signs to the things signified—to see beyond the here and now and glimpse the divine mysteries that will one day be fully visible to us in heaven (I Jn 3:2) but even now are truly present in the Church.

We may hear the story of the great flood and, through instruction, prayer, and meditation, discern the saving waters of baptism. But further, we may see beyond the sign of baptism and discern the work of the Holy Spirit, because the third person of the Blessed Trinity *is* the ultimate reality signified and conveyed by the waters of baptism.

For even Jesus' miracles—great as they were—served primarily as "signs." That is the word St. John used to describe them (see, for example, Jn 2:11 and 4:54). They were real events, and they were momentous, but still they pointed beyond themselves, to a divine and transcendent reality. Consider Jesus' healing of the paralyzed man (Mk 2:3–12). Our Lord made it clear that curing paralysis was a lesser deed than the forgiveness of sins. The physical healing was simply an outward sign of the greater healing, the inner, spiritual healing. The physical cure, after all, was a temporary reprieve; eventually the man's life would run its natural course, and he would suffer and die. The spiritual healing, however, could last even beyond death; it made for a new creation, an act possible by no one but God (Mk 2:7).

Jesus has given us the privilege of sharing in the life and saving actions of God. At the Last Supper, he spoke of his miraculous signs and then promised his apostles: "Truly, truly, I say to you, he who believes in me will also do the works that I do; and greater works than these will he do" (Jn 14:12). Though the apostles did perform miracles during their ministry, they did nothing that exceeded Jesus' miracles in grandeur. So what could he have meant?

He meant the sacraments.

The early Christians believed in the sacraments. They believed that the sacraments not only spoke *about* Jesus' divine power—but rather they *spoke Jesus' divine power.* All words signify things. Yet, in the Gospels, Jesus' word brought about the realities it signified. He spoke and demons were cast out, people were cured of their illnesses, raging winds and waters were stilled, the dead were raised. That same divine Word still has the power to transform the things of creation and the moments of our lives. It does so through the ministry of the Church, which uses the stuff of the earth—bread and wine, gestures and postures, oil and water—to bring holiness into our lives. This happens in the sacraments, which the ancient Church referred to as "mysteries." In the fifth century, Pope St. Leo the Great said: "What was visible in our Savior has passed over into his mysteries." Thus, mystagogy is rooted in God's grace: his power to change us.

That power is hidden to our natural senses. Mystagogy, on the other hand, is the Church's traditional way of revealing it to our mind and spirit. It is the saints' way of revealing the divine love that abides behind the symbols, the divine life that lives beyond the signs. In the holy things of our tradition, material objects show us immaterial realities—temporal events disclose eternal mysteries.

Mystagogy means leading believers into a real communion, a real sharing, in the saving mysteries celebrated in the symbols and rituals of the Church's worship. Pope Benedict XVI once said: "The mature fruit of mystagogy is an awareness that one's life is being progressively transformed by the holy mysteries being celebrated . . . mak[ing] him a 'new creation.'"

LIVING THE MYSTERIES

For the early Christians, the mystery of Christ was not limited to the sacramental rituals. It touched also upon morals and everyday life. It was God's "plan for the fullness of time," after all, "to unite all things in him, things in heaven and things on earth" (Eph 1:10). In Christ "all things were created, in heaven and on earth, visible and invisible . . . all things were created through him and for him . . . and in him all things hold together" (Col 1:16–17).

Thus, in Christ, all the things of the earth become signposts pointing us to God. The things of the earth are not to be despised, but rather sanctified, raised up, made holy by holy use. In the Mass we offer God the "work of human hands." In our work we do the same. We do no less in our devotion. We pray, according to our customs, as the early Christians did, with sacraments as well as *sacramentals.*

What is a sacramental?

It is any object set apart and blessed by the Church to lead us to good thoughts and increase our devotion. A sacramental is *like* a sacrament in that it is a means of grace and an outward sign of an invisible mystery of faith. It is also *unlike* a sacrament in many ways. Sacraments were instituted by Christ, while sacramentals are established by the Church. Sacraments convey grace *directly* in our souls, while sacramentals do so *indirectly,* by leading us to devotion and providing us an occasion when we may respond to God's grace.

This idea is as old as the Church. In the fourth century St. Gregory of Nyssa preached a splendid homily about this *sacramental principle.* He began by praising God for the power he gave to ordinary things: water in baptism, bread and wine in the Mass, oil in anointing, the press of the bishop's hands in ordination. "There are many things that appear to be contemptible," he said, "but accomplish mighty works." Drawing from the Old Testament, he noted the common items that God had invested with miraculous power: Moses' wooden staff, Elijah's mantle of rough cloth, and the bones of the dead Elisha.

St. Gregory saw that such a dispensation of power had not only continued in his own day, but increased many times over. So it continues into our times, too, offering us manifold graces. In fact, those three examples he gave are the remote ancestors of practices that continue into our own day, practices we'll examine in this book: the veneration of the cross, the wearing of the brown scapular, and the honor we give to the relics of the saints.

DISTINCT POSSIBILITIES

For Catholics, sacraments and sacramentals are unmistakable signs of life. Both are part of this book, as both should be part of our everyday living and loving.

Jesus' own devotional life was very rich. He took part in pilgrimages and festivals. He prayed spontaneously and formally. He prayed kneeling and standing and prostrate. He worshipped alone, with congregations, and with friends. He recited the Scriptures. He went on silent retreats, away from the bustle and distractions of the world.

It is our privilege to imitate him in that beautiful variety, and our tradition gives us many ways of doing so. It's true that not all prayers and devotions are created equal. As we take up the customs of our Catholic faith, it's important that we distinguish between those that are essential and those that we may choose or reject with Christian freedom. We have a strict obligation to be baptized and go to Mass on Sundays and holy days of obligation (see Jn 3:5 and 6:53). We are not obliged, however, to say the Rosary, use holy water, or pray novenas. Nevertheless, sometimes it's the nonessentials that transform a house into a true home. Yes, we need the bricks and mortar to build up a functional shelter; but life is a whole lot richer when we can also smell the aroma of dinner cooking in the kitchen and hear the babbling of small children in the living room. These time-tested devotions really do help to make our faith a *life* and our Church a *home.*

Still, I know that some people will dismiss all habits of piety, objecting that they're just rote and routine habits. They are indeed habits, and we can indeed make them rote and routine. But those qualities, by themselves, are not bad. Rote and routine are quite good, in fact, when we apply them to lawn care, car care, musical performance, or personal hygiene. I maintain, with Catholic tradition, that routines of prayer, when offered from the heart, can be very good for the soul. They are like beautiful music or gardens tended with care—rote habits rooted in love.

Others will object that these actions are medieval superstitions or attempts to manipulate God. But that's simply not so. By offering our prayers, we're not getting God to do our bidding; we're allowing God to have his way. These ways of prayer are divine mercies, a language God fosters so we will speak with him regularly and often, whether we feel like it or not. Our devotions are not primarily what we do for God—he does not need our praise or our incense—but rather what he does for us. These modes of communication conform remarkably well to the human mind and body, which God himself created for his glory.

How the Book Works

In this book, we'll examine different traditional practices of the Church.

In each chapter we'll look at the deep biblical and historical roots of a particular Catholic custom. We'll find answers to common objections raised by non-Catholics, and we'll try to clear up some common misconceptions. Each chapter concludes with a

"Ponder in Your Heart" section. The title refers to Luke's description of the Blessed Virgin: "Mary kept all these things, pondering them in her heart" (Lk 2:19). I'm hoping that you and I can imitate her as we ponder the words of Christian history's great teachers, thinkers, and saints. I chose these "Ponder" passages from the tradition. I've included these passages from many of the centuries from Jesus' to our own. Taken all together, they make an important point: that these doctrines and devotions are not my inventions, that they have been confirmed by tradition, and that they work. They've helped other Catholics, many Catholics, down through the centuries, mark their way to heaven. I chose passages from a variety of authors. I chose the passages I have found most helpful.

The idea here is to heighten our awareness of our faith, to make our devotions as *everyday* as possible. We want to form good *habits* of prayer—or, to use the more intimidating modern term: *disciplines* of prayer. The sacramental principle works so well because it presupposes the fundamental reality of human nature: we are composed of body and soul, a material body and a spiritual soul. What we do to one component profoundly affects the other. What we do with our body, our senses, provides the foundation for our spiritual growth. Grace builds on nature.

There are many good, natural reasons to take up the traditional methods of prayer. Physiologists recognize that they relax our bodies, reduce our stress levels, and unfurrow our brows. They also burn durable neural pathways. Anyone who has spent time by the deathbeds of faithful Catholics can testify, as I can: there are certain devotions that seem fairly consistently to remain to the very end of consciousness, even when much else has vanished from memory. I have a dear friend whose mother survived a stroke with little left but the ability to recite the Rosary—a habit ingrained over a long lifetime. It proved to be her path to recovery. I could tell hundreds of stories like this one.

So it makes no sense to defer the disciplines of prayer till we're older. First, we may not have the luxury of getting older. But even if we do, we may not have the health, memory, or freedom necessary to establish new habits.

It may sound cliché, but we don't know what lies ahead for us. We do know that we'll suffer, you and I, because that's part of life, even life in Christ. But God has provided for those times. He and his Church have given us a storehouse of tradition—methods and counsel that have proven reliable over the course of millennia, through the lives of countless ordinary Christians, through economic depression and natural disasters, through persecution and war. Now that's what I call research and development!

In every trial, God will "provide the way of escape, that you may be able to endure it" (1 Cor 10:13). Even amid the most extraordinary circumstances, we can escape to God, we can endure, and we can prevail, using the most ordinary means of prayer. It is a very good thing if all we need to do is touch a bead or feel the wool of a scapular in order to turn our thoughts to God, because we may come to moments when that's all we *can* do.

I pray you'll pray these prayers, as well as you can, and ask the Holy Spirit and your guardian angel to make up for whatever you lack.

As you pray, please remember to pray for this author—who promises to pray for his readers!

Back to the Cross

Oh, yes, I promised to finish my story about my dissertation.

I returned home saying the Rosary, by way of my neighborhood's darkened streets, but I felt as if it was broad daylight. Once back in my office, I returned to the biblical text—which I had read hundreds and possibly thousands of times—and read it as if for the first time. In fact, I encountered it as if I were the first person reading it. In the original Greek I saw connections that had not made it cleanly into the English and Latin translations.

To cut to the chase: I found a solution that, till then, had appeared nowhere else in the commentaries. I finished my dissertation and defended it successfully. I wrote up my findings and published them in a major scholarly journal.

Twelve years after that fateful, faithful night, I was attending a professional conference, the annual meeting of the Society of Biblical Literature, when a scholar I respect took me aside and asked: "How does it feel to have nailed it?"

I had no idea what he was talking about.

"How does it feel," he asked, "to have found the interpretation that had been lost to the ages?"

Then I knew what he meant, and my eyes welled up.

I told him the story about a night long ago, a wall too high for me to scale. I told him of my journey to the cross. I wanted him to know the way, in case he, too, should find himself at a wall.

I want the same for you, and that's the reason for the rest of this book.

I

Life Begins

1.

....

HOLY WATER

We begin in water.

That's how the book of Genesis poetically depicts the creation of the universe: "darkness was upon the face of the deep; and the Spirit of God was moving over the face of the waters . . . And God said, 'Let there be a firmament in the midst of the waters, and let it separate the waters from the waters'" (Gen 1:2, 6).

As it was in the cosmic, so it is in our personal beginnings: we assume our human form in the amniotic sac, "bag of waters," in the womb. In the order of nature, birth begins when a mother's "water breaks."

So with water we begin our visits to church. We dip a hand into a holy-water font, and we bless ourselves.

There has been a watermark on Christian prayer since the earliest days of the Church. At the end of the second century, a North African theologian named Tertullian mentions the custom of symbolically cleansing one's hands before lifting them in prayer. It was a Jewish custom that predated the coming of Our Lord, and it may be what St. Paul was referring to when he wrote to Timothy: "I desire then that in every place the men should pray, lifting holy hands" or "pure hands" (I Tim 2:8). The historian Eusebius, writing around A.D. 320, describes a church in Tyre that had flowing fountains at its entrance, where the faithful might purify their hands.

We use water to mark our beginnings because God does. We find ample evidence of this in both nature and Scripture. When the world was lost to sin and needed cleansing and rebirth, God sent a great flood, and from that flood the family of Noah found new life. When Israel emerged from slavery as a unified nation, it first had to pass through the waters of the Red Sea. When the chosen people established their places of worship—first the tabernacle and then the Temple—they constructed them with bronze basins for washing upon entry.

St. Thomas Aquinas taught that water has been a natural sacrament since the dawn of creation. In the age of nature—from Adam through the patriarchs—water refreshed and cleansed humankind. In the age of Law—the time of Moses—water provided a spiritual rebirth for Israel as the nation began its journey to the promised land. With Jesus, however, came the age of grace; and from that time onward water received the divine power of the Word made flesh. Though babies had always been born through "water," now grown men and women could be "born of water and the Holy Spirit" (Jn 3:5). The Church Fathers taught that Jesus, by descending into the waters of the River Jordan, had sanctified the waters of the world. He made them living and life-giving (see Jn 4:10–14). He made them a source of *supernatural* regeneration, refreshment, and cleansing.

While we are on earth, we know spiritual things by means of

sensible signs. It is only in glory that we will see divine things as they are, without their sacramental veils. According to St. Thomas, water ultimately "signifies the grace of the Holy Spirit . . . For the Holy Spirit is the unfailing fountain from whom all gifts of grace flow." The book of Revelation confirms this, as it presents the Spirit's grace as a "river of the water of life, bright as crystal, flowing from the throne of God and of the Lamb" (Rev 22:1).

Through history and through the cosmos, God has spoken with a voice that is "like the sound of many waters" (Rev 1:15). All the many sacred meanings of water we take for our own and claim as our inheritance—whenever we bless ourselves with holy water.

"Beloved, we are God's children now," born of water and the Spirit. "And everyone who thus hopes in him purifies himself as he is pure" (1 Jn 3:2-3).

This simple action, which even the smallest children love to do, is a reminder and a renewal of our baptism. It is a refreshment, too, providing relief from the oppression of evil. St. Teresa of Avila wrote that "there is nothing the devils flee from more—without returning—than holy water."

Holy water is ordinary water that has been blessed for devotional use by a priest. We bless ourselves with holy water at church. Most churches also provide a dispenser so that parishioners can draw water to take home with them. Some Catholic families keep a little holy-water font at the entryway to every bedroom. I keep a bottle of the stuff in my office at all times.

We need do no more with it than splash a few drops on ourselves. It is customary to pronounce a blessing in the name of the Holy Trinity, too, and trace the outline of a cross with our right hand.

That's enough for now. We'll save the rest for the next chapter.

Ponder in Your Heart

King and Lord of all things and maker of the world:
you gave salvation freely to all created nature by the descent of your only-begotten Jesus Christ. You redeemed
all that you created by the coming of your ineffable
Word. See now from heaven, and look upon these waters, and fill them with the Holy Spirit. Let your ineffable Word come to be in them and tranform their
energy and cause them to be generative, as being filled
with your grace . . . As your only-begotten Word coming down upon the waters of the Jordan rendered them
holy, so now may he descend on these and make them
holy and spiritual.

—Blessing of Water, from the sacramentary of
St. Serapion of Egypt, fourth century

2.

THE SIGN OF THE CROSS

What water is to elements, the Sign of the Cross is to gestures. Cardinal Joseph Ratzinger (the future Pope Benedict XVI) once wrote: "The most basic Christian gesture in prayer is and always will be the Sign of the Cross."

This is the most common prayer of Christians, and it has been since the founding of the Church. St. Paul speaks of the cross in almost all his New Testament letters: "But far be it from me to glory except in the cross of our Lord Jesus Christ, by which the world has been crucified to me, and I to the world" (Gal 6:14).

We could fill a book with the early Christians' testimonies to this practice. It was their favorite devotion as it required no special knowledge or skill. You didn't have to be literate to make the Sign of the Cross, or rich enough to own a book of instructions. All you needed was one working finger. Martyrs made the Sign as they were taken to their death. Even Julian, the notoriously ex-Christian emperor, fell back to tracing the Sign whenever he felt oppressed by demons.

It is mentioned everywhere because it was practiced everywhere. At the end of the second century, Tertullian proclaimed: "In all our travels and movements, in all our coming in and going out, in putting on our shoes, at the bath, at the table, in lighting our candles, in lying down, in sitting down, whatever task occupies us, we mark our forehead with the sign of the cross." Tertullian praised his wife for her virtues, her beauty, and her wardrobe, but preeminently because she made the Sign of the Cross over her body and over her bed before retiring for the night.

The earliest accounts suggest that Christians traced the cross with their thumb upon their forehead. They also traced it on objects, such as food, and over the sacramental elements: bread, wine, oil, and water.

Over the centuries the faithful have developed many ways of doing it. In the Western churches, we bless ourselves with our open right hand, touching our fingertips to the forehead, then the breastbone, then the left shoulder, and finally the right shoulder. Some interpret the five open fingers as a sign of the Five Wounds of Christ.

In the Mass, just before the Gospel, we use another form as well: a "Small Sign of the Cross," in which we trace with our thumb a cruciform on our forehead and lips, and over our heart. When the priest or deacon does this, we can sometimes hear him say quietly: "The Lord be in my heart and on my lips that I may worthily proclaim his holy Gospel." People who use the Small Sign in private devotions sometimes offer it with the Latin prayer *Per signum crucis de inimicis nostris libera nos Deus noster* ("By the sign of the cross, our God, deliver us from our enemies").

Christians of the Eastern churches have their own way of making the Sign. Their placement of fingers turns the hand into a virtual catechism. They join the thumb, index, and middle finger at the fingertips. The three fingers together represent the Trinity in unity. The remaining two fingers—pinky and ring—are pressed together against the palm, and they together symbolize the hypostatic union: the unity of Jesus' human and divine natures.

Some people, in the East and the West, keep the custom of kissing their fingers at the conclusion of the Sign.

Worldwide and throughout history, there are countless variations on the practice and its interpretation. One of my favorite explanations comes from my patron saint, Francis de Sales:

> We raise the hand first to the forehead, saying, "In the name of the Father," to signify that the Father is the first person of the Most Holy Trinity, of whom the Son is begotten and from whom the Holy Spirit proceeds. Then saying, "And the Son," the hand is lowered to the breast, to express that the Son proceeds from the Father, who sent him down to the womb of the Virgin. Then the hand is moved from the left shoulder or side to the right, while saying, "and of the Holy Spirit," thereby signifying that the Holy Spirit, as the third person of the Holy Trinity, proceeds from the Father and the Son, that he is the love that unites both, and that we, through his grace, partake of the fruits of the passion. Accordingly the Sign of the Cross is a brief declaration of our faith in the three great mysteries: of our faith in the Blessed Trinity, in the passion of Christ, and in the forgiveness of sin, by which we pass from the left side of curse to the right of blessing.

The Trinity and the cross: it's not an accident of piety that these two themes converge in the words and gesture of the Church's most fundamental and most popular prayer.

The cross is an image in time of the Trinity's life in eternity. On the cross, Jesus Christ gave himself entirely. He held nothing back.

Such is the self-giving of the Son for the Father, the Father for the Son. Each makes a complete and loving gift of his life to the other, and that gift, that life, that love, is the Holy Spirit. The sign of that love in the world is the Sign of the Cross.

At the end of his struggle, Jesus gave up his Spirit (Jn 19:30) as he pronounced his work "finished," accomplished, fulfilled. When we make the Sign of the Cross, we correspond to that grace. We receive the love he gives. We take on that Spirit as we take up his cross. We see Jesus give himself in love, and we say "Amen!" We accept that life as our own.

It's no small thing we do when we make the Sign of the Cross. It should take our breath away—but only so that we can be filled up with another wind, another breath: the Spirit of God.

This is the life we received in baptism, when we were marked with the Sign and saved from our sins. The early Christians compared this to the mark on the brow of Cain (Gen 4:15), which protected him from the punishment he deserved. They saw it foreshadowed also in the mark of blood on the doorposts that saved the firstborn sons of the Israelites at the Passover (Ex 12:7). They saw it even more vividly depicted in the oracle of the prophet Ezekiel, who saw that the righteous in Jerusalem would one day be saved because of a "mark upon the foreheads" (Ez 9:4). What was that mark? According to the ancient rabbis, it was *tav*, the last letter of the Hebrew alphabet, which in ancient times was drawn as a cross. In the New Testament, in the book of Revelation, St. John saw the faithful in heaven distinguished by this Sign on their foreheads (Rev 14:1, 22:4).

The custom has passed down through the ages, and indeed it will always be with us. In his groundbreaking work on Sacred Tradition, St. Basil the Great identified it as a hallmark of the apostolic faith. It is honored even in heaven, and even by the greatest of saints. At Lourdes, France, in 1858, when the Virgin Mary first appeared to little Bernadette Soubirous, before she uttered a single word, she made the Sign of the Cross.

This simplest gesture is the richest of creeds. It encompasses the infinite. It proclaims the Trinity, the incarnation, and our redemption. It is, in the words of Cardinal Ratzinger, a "summing up and re-acceptance of our baptism." As Pope Benedict XVI, he added: "Making the Sign of the Cross . . . means saying a visible and public 'yes' to the One who died and rose for us, to God who in the humility and weakness of his love is the Almighty, stronger than all the power and intelligence of the world."

Ponder in Your Heart

When we cross ourselves, let it be with a real Sign of the Cross. Instead of a small cramped gesture that gives no notion of its meaning, let us make a large unhurried sign, from forehead to breast, from shoulder to shoulder, consciously feeling how it includes the whole of us, our thoughts, our attitudes, our body and soul, every part of us at once, how it consecrates and sanctifies us . . .

Think of these things when you make the Sign of the Cross. It is the holiest of all signs . . . Let it take in your whole being—body, soul, mind, will, thoughts, feelings, your doing and not-doing—and by signing it with the cross strengthen and consecrate the whole in the strength of Christ, in the name of the triune God.

—Romano Guardini, twentieth century

3.

··

BAPTISM

You've probably seen greeting cards that claim "Life begins at forty" or thirty or fifty.

Don't believe them. Life begins at baptism. Baptism is the quintessential "sign of life." Jesus himself spoke of baptism in terms of strict obligation: "unless one is born of water and the Spirit, he cannot enter the kingdom of God" (Jn 3:5). Baptism was the substance of his final earthly command: "Go therefore and make disciples of all nations, baptizing them in the name of the Father and of the Son and of the Holy Spirit" (Mt 28:19). When new believers asked St. Peter, the first pope, what they should do, he infallibly declared: "Repent, and be baptized every one of you" (Acts 2:38).

Just as our natural living cannot proceed without a birth, so our supernatural life cannot proceed without our baptism.

Before our baptism, we may have a beating heart and a lively mind. We may even have an important job and many friends—so that no one would ever dare to tell us to "get a life." Yet, until we're baptized, we don't have the kind of life Jesus talked about when he said: "I am the way, and the truth, and the life; no one comes to the Father, but by me" (Jn 14:6).

His statement is curious, because people can indeed go to God without going by way of Jesus. Even pagans can. St. Paul said so in his Letter to the Romans: "what can be known about God is plain to them, because God has shown it to them" (1:19–20). But here's the difference: they cannot know him as *Father*. And that is the essence of Christianity.

It's easy for us to take God's fatherhood for granted. It has become a rather bland cliché: God is our Father, and we're all brothers and sisters, so let's all get along. We forget that this assertion was once enough to get a man killed: "This was why the Jews sought all the more to kill [Jesus], because he . . . called God his Father" (Jn 5:18). Even today, Muslims consider it blasphemy to attribute fatherhood to God.

Children, whether natural or adopted, must share the same nature as their parents. I might feel an extreme fondness for my pets, but I cannot make them my children, because they do not possess human nature.

Thus, when a person calls God "Father," he is—as Jesus' contemporaries rightly observed—"making himself equal with God" (Jn 5:18), because a father and child must share the same nature.

God's fatherhood is the truth at the heart of Jesus' gospel of salvation. When we are born anew in baptism, we are born not of human parentage, but heavenly: "See what love the Father has given us, that we should be called children of God; and so we are . . . we are God's children now; it does not yet appear what we shall be, but we know that when he appears we shall be like him" (1 Jn 3:1–2).

What can all this mean?

Theologians since ancient times have described our salvation as

a "marvelous exchange." In Jesus, God became what we are so that
we might become what he is. The Son of God became the Son of
Man so that the children of men might become children of God.
Through baptism we become "partakers of the divine nature"
(2 Pt 1:4). We are baptized *into* Christ, so that we can live *in* him.
The early Christians daringly called this process our *divinization* or
deification. It is, like natural birth, a pure gift, nothing we could ever
accomplish or earn for ourselves. We become by grace what God is
by nature. That is why God became a man, and that is why he gave
us baptism.

Such was God's intention from the beginning of time. The
apostles found the waters of baptism abundantly foretold in the
Old Testament (see chapter 1). St. Paul, however, saw baptism also
as a fulfillment of the ancient Hebrews' practice of circumcising
all newborn males: "you were circumcised with a circumcision
made without hands, by putting off the body of flesh in the circumcision of Christ; and you were buried with him in baptism"
(Col 2:11–12). The circumcision of infants, then, prefigured the
baptism of those who would be "newborn" in Christ. The old rite
marked a child's "birth" as a son of Abraham; the new rite marks
the still greater birth of a child of God.

To be precise: with circumcision, a boy entered into God's
covenant with the family of Abraham. A covenant is a legal action
based upon an oath; its purpose is to create a family bond between
formerly unrelated persons. Marriage is a covenant. Adoption is a
covenant. God made a covenant with Abraham, so that Abraham's
descendants through Isaac would be God's family on earth.

Circumcision was the preeminent sign of the Old Covenant (see
Acts 7:8). God welcomed newborns into Israel by means of ritual
circumcision—though adult males, too, would undergo the painful
rite if they chose to convert to Judaism.

From the beginning the Church, in turn, received infants and adults—and all ages in between—into the family of God by means of baptism, the "circumcision made without hands."

Circumcision was painful. It was costly. It was a down payment in blood that served as a pledge of one's entire life. Yet membership in God's family was well worth the price.

With baptism the rewards are even greater, but the cost is greater, too. St. Ambrose of Milan, writing in the fourth century, put it this way. A man who underwent circumcision endured pain in one part of the body, for a brief time. Yet baptism, he said, is "the sacrament of the cross." Whether an infant or an adult, the Christian who has been "baptized into Christ Jesus" has been "baptized into his death" (Rom 6:3). That death means a new life for us, a "new creation" (2 Cor 5:17; Gal 6:15).

Salvation has not exempted us from suffering. Christ is our "pioneer," precisely because he has suffered (Heb 2:10 and 12:2). A pioneer is not the last to enter a new territory, but the first. He has gone before us, to serve as a model for imitation, and to empower us to follow after him. We live the life of children of God when we live the life of Christ, when we live as he lived, when we suffer as he suffered. By the power of our baptism, we can live his life for all eternity in heaven. For us as for him, it starts here and now. By baptism, we are "conformed to the image of [God's] Son" (Rom 8:29). We are, here and now, "being changed into his likeness from one degree of glory to another" (2 Cor 3:18). This happens not *in spite of* our suffering, but *through* our suffering—which, because of that "marvelous exchange," works in us with divine power, redemptive power.

We must not allow ourselves to be lulled by the clichés about God's fatherhood. The doctrine of baptism is so rich, so radical, and so revolutionary that it was baffling to Nicodemus—who was perhaps the most learned and clever of Jesus' friends (see Jn 3:1–15). Jesus told Nicodemus, in so many words, that he would need the grace of baptism in order to understand the new birth of baptism. The early Church followed the Lord in imparting the doctrine of baptism to adults only *after* they had been baptized. Only then were they capable of approaching the mysteries—and living the mysteries, because baptism had (and has) profound implications for Christian moral life.

For we the baptized are living "in Christ" (see Rom 8:1), and Christ is living in us (Gal 2:20). We are sons and daughters in the eternal Son of God. Though Christ had the "form of God" (Phil 2:6), he poured himself out to take on a human "form" (2:7)—again, so that we might be in him and he in us. "So you also must consider yourselves dead to sin and alive to God in Christ Jesus. Let not sin therefore reign in your mortal bodies, to make you obey their passions. Do not yield your members to sin as instruments of wickedness, but yield yourselves to God as men who have been brought from death to life, and your members to God as instruments of righteousness. For sin will have no dominion over you, since you are not under law but under grace" (Rom 6:11–14).

Baptism is not merely a ceremony, not merely a rite of passage. It is our entry into a New Covenant bond, a new family, a new life, a new birth, a new creation. "We are Christians because of a covenant," said the theologian Romano Guardini. Yet he also lamented that "it is strange how completely the idea of the covenant has vanished from the Christian consciousness. We do mention it, but it seems to have lost its meaning for us." We should take every care to understand our baptism and never underestimate it—and not only our own baptism, but those of our friends and especially our children and godchildren (what a great and sweet responsibility that is). Do you know your baptismal day as well as you know your birthday? Do you mark it in some special way?

Ponder in Your Heart

In considering . . . the gift which comes from baptism, the apostle Peter breaks out into song: "Blessed be the God and Father of our Lord Jesus Christ! By his great mercy we have been born anew to a living hope through the resurrection of Jesus Christ from the dead, and to an inheritance which is imperishable, undefiled and un-fading" (I Pt 1:3–4). And he calls Christians those who have been "born anew, not of perishable seed but of imperishable, through the living and abiding word of God" (I Pt 1:23).

With baptism we become children of God in his only-begotten Son, Jesus Christ. Rising from the waters of the baptismal font, every Christian hears again the voice that was once heard on the banks of the Jordan River: "You are my beloved Son; with you I am well pleased" (Lk 3:22). From this comes the understand-ing that one has been brought into association with the beloved Son, becoming a child of adoption (cf. Gal 4:4–7) and a brother or sister of Christ. In this way the eternal plan of the Father for each person is realized in history. . .

St. Maximus, Bishop of Turin, in addressing those who had received the holy anointing of baptism, re-peats the same sentiments: "Ponder the honor that has made you sharers in this mystery!" All the baptized are

invited to hear once again the words of St. Augustine:
"Let us rejoice and give thanks: we have not only become Christians, but Christ himself . . . Stand in awe
and rejoice: We have become Christ."

—Pope John Paul II, twentieth century

4.

The Mass

Long before the New Testament books were written—before any churches were built, before the first disciple died as a martyr for the faith—the Mass was the center of life for the Church.

St. Luke sums it up in the Acts of the Apostles: "And they devoted themselves to the apostles' teaching and fellowship, to the breaking of bread and the prayers" (Acts 2:42). Luke manages to get so much detail into that single sentence. The first Christians were eucharistic by nature: they gathered for "the breaking of the bread and the prayers." They were formed by the Word of God, the "apostles' teaching." When they met as a Church, their worship culminated in "fellowship"—the Greek word is *koinonia*, communion.

The Mass was the center of life for the disciples of Jesus, and so it has ever been. Even today, the Mass is where we experience the apostolic teaching and communion, the breaking of the bread and the prayers.

St. Luke focuses primarily on the externals, which are mighty by themselves, but the Mass is still so much more.

The first Christians were Jews, living in a Jewish culture, steeped in Jewish forms of worship. They saw the Eucharist as the fulfillment of all the rites of the Old Covenant. Jesus' sacrifice had rendered Israel's ceremonial laws obsolete, but it had not dispensed entirely with ritual worship. Jesus himself established rites for the New Covenant: baptism (Mt 28:19), for example, and sacramental absolution (Jn 20:22–23). He reserved the greatest solemnity, however, for the Eucharist (Lk 22:20).

The liturgy of the new covenant had been foreshadowed in the rituals of the old. The Gospels make an explicit connection between the Mass and the Passover meal (Lk 22:15). The Epistle to the Hebrews sees the Mass in light of the Temple's animal sacrifices (Heb 13:10). Many modern scholars have noted parallels between the Mass and the most commonly offered sacrifice of Jesus' day: the thank-offering (in Hebrew, *todah*). The todah was a sacrificial meal of bread and wine, shared with his friends, given in thanksgiving for God's deliverance. The Talmud records the ancient rabbis' teaching that, when the Messiah has come, "all sacrifices will cease except the todah sacrifice. This will never cease in all eternity." When the Jews translated their Scriptures into Greek, they rendered the word *todah* as *eucharistia,* the word from which we get "Eucharist."

All of Israel's traditions of worship were like mighty rivers that flowed into the infinite ocean of adoration that Jesus established for the Church. There they did not vanish, but found completion.

Many years before he became pope, Cardinal Joseph Ratzinger wrote of yet another notion from ancient Jewish ritual. *Chaburah* was the word used to describe the fellowship shared by members of God's covenant family. They shared *chaburah* with one another. They ate *chaburah* meals together. On the eve of a Sabbath or holy day, a rabbi would customarily share such a supper with his disciples. When Jews translated the word into Greek, they rendered it as *koinonia*, communion. The divine covenant brought about powerful fellowship among the people of God.

But the Jews stopped short of describing any *chaburah* between God and human beings. They believed such communion to be impossible. The very idea would be an affront to God's transcendence. God, after all, is infinite, perfect, and all-good. We are finite, imperfect, and sinful. How could two parties so vastly different enjoy communion with one another, when one party is so clearly unworthy?

God himself disregarded the threat of defilement; and by means of the new covenant, he himself established communion with his people: all of us in the Church, and each of us in the Church. This may be why the language of "covenant," which is everywhere in the Old Testament, appears rarely in the New Testament; it is replaced by the language of communion. The Mass, said Jesus, "is the new covenant in my blood" (I Cor 11:25); but now, in this *New* Covenant, he has raised the stakes. He has given the Mass as "a communion [*koinonia*] in the blood of Christ" (I Cor 10:16).

The apostles made clear that Jesus' salvation had shattered not only the boundaries between Israel and the nations, but also between God and the world. Yes, fellowship was now possible among all peoples, both Jews and Gentiles. God's family would at last be universal.

Now, too, God himself would share communion with his people. Our life in Christ is our sharing, our participation, our communion in God's life. It is, at last, *chaburah* between God and mankind.

Ancient Israel had always considered its earthly liturgy to be a divinely inspired imitation of heavenly worship. What the priests did in the Temple was an earthly imitation of what the angels did in heaven. Yet it was still only an imitation, only a *shadow*.

By assuming human flesh, the eternal Son of God brought heaven to earth. No longer must the people of God worship in imitation of angels. In the liturgy of the new covenant, Christ himself presides, and we not only imitate the angels; we participate with them. Through the Mass—and in every Mass—there is *communion* between heaven and earth.

We can see that reality most vividly in the book of Revelation, where the Church on earth gathers at the altar with the angels and saints in heaven . . . where we hear the "Holy, Holy, Holy," the "Lamb of God," the Amen and Alleluia and other familiar songs . . . where priests serve in vestments in a sanctuary adorned with candles . . . where chalices are poured out and worshippers feast on "hidden manna." It is, I believe, no accident that the Apocalypse divides neatly into two halves, the first consisting of readings and the second of the "marriage supper of the Lamb." This structure corresponds to the most ancient order of divine worship.

For Christian liturgy still follows the basic pattern of Old Testament worship: a service that includes both the reading of the Word of God and the offering of sacrifice. Jesus himself followed that outline when he appeared to his disciples on the road to Emmaus: "Beginning with Moses and all the prophets, he interpreted to them in all the Scriptures the things concerning himself"; and then they knew him "in the breaking of the bread" (Lk 24:27, 35). In the Mass, we still hear the New Testament readings along with the Old Testament, and we view all the history of salvation in light of its ultimate fulfillment—in light of Christ. In the Mass, we still know Jesus, really present, in the breaking of the bread.

The New Covenant is indeed something new, great, and glorious. Yet we should not forget its continuity with the past. Israel's ritual worship was ordered to covenant remembrance (in reading) and renewal (in sacrifice). Christian worship, too, is a remembrance of God's mighty works in history, especially Jesus' saving passion and glorification. The Christian Eucharist remains both a covenant renewal and a thanksgiving for God's continued presence among his people.

Now that presence is a true communion. This fact astonished the early Christians, who proclaimed that the Mass was heaven on earth, and the earthly altar was the same as the heavenly. The Mass is the coming of Christ we all await. God comes to us in true communion, and the "marvelous exchange" takes on a flesh-and-blood dimension. We are God's children now, and "the children share in flesh and blood" (Heb 2:14).

This does not mean that the parishioners around us will remind us of Raphael's cherubs. Sometimes they'll have screaming babies with pungent diapers. It does not mean that the choir at St. Dymphna's Parish will ever sing on key. Nor does it mean Father's preaching will be consistently compelling.

It means what the incarnation has always meant: "the Word became flesh and dwelt among us" (Jn 1:14) . . . He "emptied himself" and "humbled himself" (Phil 2:7–8) . . . "the dwelling of God is with men. He will dwell with them, and they shall be his people, and God himself will be with them" (Rev 21:3).

In the Mass, he is "God with us" (Mt 1:23) where we are, as we are, though he loves us too much to leave us that way. Through the Eucharist, he makes us what he is; where he is he transforms us from glory to glory.

Ponder in Your Heart

Here we must apply our minds attentively, and consider the apostolic wisdom; for again he shows the change in the priesthood, who "serve a copy and shadow of the heavenly sanctuary" (Heb 8:5).

What are the heavenly things he speaks of here? The spiritual things. For although they are done on earth, yet nevertheless they are worthy of the heavens. For when our Lord Jesus Christ lies slain [as a sacrifice], when the Spirit is with us, when he who sits at the right hand of the Father is here, when sons are made by the washing, when they are fellow-citizens of those in heaven, when we have a country, and a city, and citizenship there, when we are strangers to things here, how can all these be other than heavenly things?

But what! Are not our hymns heavenly? Do not we also who are below utter together with them the same things that the divine choirs of bodiless powers sing above? Is not the altar also heavenly? How? It has nothing carnal, all spiritual things become the offerings. The sacrifice does not disperse into ashes, or into smoke, or into steamy savor, it makes the things placed there bright and splendid. How again can the rites that we celebrate be other than heavenly? For when he says, "If you forgive the sins of any, they are forgiven; if you retain the sins of any, they are retained" (Jn 20:23), when they have the keys of heaven, how can all be other than heavenly? . . .

No, one would not be wrong in saying even this; for the Church is heavenly, and is nothing else than heaven.

—St. John Chrysostom, fifth century

5.

....

GUARDIAN ANGELS

Among the liveliest traditions in the ancient Church was devotion to the guardian angels. Yet it is something that modern readers often miss. The dramatic plot of the Acts of the Apostles is borne forward by the action of angels. Angels set the apostles free from prison (5:19, 12:7). An angel guides Philip from Jerusalem to Gaza for his fateful meeting with the Ethiopian court official (8:26). Angels bring about the meeting of Peter and Cornelius (10:3–5). My favorite instance is when Peter arrives at a house-church, and the people assume that it's *not* Peter, but rather his angel (12:15)!

The story of the Church moves forward with the guidance, protection, and assistance of angels. So do our lives. The early Christians knew this. That's why they could easily mistake a man for his guardian angel. Since Peter was imprisoned, they would naturally be surprised to find him at the door, but they were *not* surprised to encounter his angel!

We need to have such faith and such a lively awareness of our guardian angels. For God has given us—each of us—the same powerful heavenly guidance, protection, and assistance.

Devotion to the angels did not arise as something new with the proclamation of the Gospel. It has always been a part of biblical religion. Angels fill the Bible, from beginning to end, Genesis to Revelation. They are key players in the drama of the Garden of Eden. They appear frequently in the life of the patriarchs: Jacob even wrestles with one. They go before the Israelites during the exodus. They deliver God's word to the prophets. The prophets themselves reveal that even *nations* have guardian angels. The book of Tobit shows us how an angel guided a young man to recover his family's fortune, discover a cure for his father's blindness, and find a beautiful and virtuous wife along the way!

The New Testament opens with an explosion of angelic activity. Neither Joseph nor Mary seems particularly surprised to receive the help of angels.

What exactly are angels? The word comes from the Greek *angelos,* which is used to translate the Hebrew *malakh.* In those languages, the words denote, literally, a "messenger"—a messenger from God. In the great tradition the term *angel* has come to apply to the entire range of bodiless, purely spiritual beings created by God. Some he created for worship at his throne. Others he also gave the power of governance over the natural powers of the universe. Some are messengers. In the Bible, they sometimes appear in human form—or even in scarifying symbolic form, with many eyes (representing their prodigious knowledge) or titanic size (representing their superhuman strength).

As we saw in the last chapter, both Jews and Christians in the ancient world kept a healthy awareness of angelic presence *especially* during their ritual worship. It is interesting to note that one of the most popular books in the community that preserved the Dead Sea Scrolls was a manual for worship called *The Angelic Liturgy*.

Still today, when we go to Mass, the congregation is never small, even if it is *nonexistent* in terms of human attendance. The angels are there, as is evident even in the words of the Mass: "And so with all the choirs of angels we sing: Holy, holy, holy . . ." The Mass itself cries out for us to be aware of our angels.

We should, of course, be particularly attentive to our own guardian angels, since they are specifically assigned to our care.

Devotion to the angels is sure to raise a condescending smile from rationalists, who will reduce it to sentimental holy cards depicting little children on a rickety bridge. Yet angels have always been part of biblical religion; and, as even secular philosophers have acknowledged, it's hard to account for the cosmos without them. The twentieth-century liberal philosopher Isaiah Berlin was fairly obsessed with the necessity of angels. The philosopher Mortimer Adler was a self-described "pagan" when he concluded that angels were part of the fabric of the universe.

If we could see things as they are, and not merely as they appear, we would find it hard to account for our lives without some understanding of the place of angels.

From the time we are smallest, each of us has a guardian angel. Jesus said: "See that you do not despise one of these little ones; for I tell you that in heaven their angels always behold the face of my Father who is in heaven" (Mt 18:10).

God gives us these guides so that we may have superhuman help on our way to heaven. Our guardian angels want to help us cooperate with the will of God, and they want to keep us from sinning. They want to help us to help others—and they want to keep us from mucking up the lives of others. Along the way, of course, they may help us to walk safely across an unsteady bridge, but only if that will accomplish God's will for us and for the world. They want the best for us, which does not always coincide with the things we desire most. The difficult fact is that what's best for us does not necessarily correspond with our comfort, health, or safety. Sometimes suffering is what's best for us, if only because it keeps us from sinning or tempting others to sin.

Still, our guardian angels do work diligently to win our trust—because that indeed is in *our* own best interest. And so they do undoubtedly help us, especially when we ask them, to find an open parking space or navigate a confusing grid of city streets. The angels follow after God's pattern of governance: they sometimes give us what we want so that we'll learn to ask for what we need.

Always remember: we are God's children now. No one spends as much on child care as God does. Why does he lavish so much on us, creating powerful pure spirits to watch over us?

Because he loves us, of course, and because he has called us all to holiness—a state that means more than mere "goodness." To be holy is to be set apart for a divine purpose, to be set apart for God. God made the Garden of Eden to be a holy place, and he positioned angels to guard it and keep it pure (Gen 3:24). When he commissioned the tabernacle and later the Jerusalem Temple, he intended these places to be his sanctuaries, and he positioned angels to guard them (Ex 25:18; I Kgs 8:6–7).

We were created to be not a random collection of carbon, hydrogen, and oxygen molecules, but as temples of the Holy Spirit (I Cor 3:16, 6:19). Our angels, like those primeval cherubim, are charged with the task of protecting the sanctuary and keeping it pure for the presence of God.

We would do well often to pray the rhyme that's taught to little children:

> *Angel of God, my guardian dear,*
> *To whom God's love commits me here:*
> *Ever this day be at my side*
> *To light and guard, to rule and guide. Amen.*

We should also know the protection of St. Michael the Archangel. He appears in Scripture as the special guardian of God's people in the Old Testament (Dan 12:1) and the New (Rev 12:7). The Church has always recognized St. Michael's role in the spiritual combat. He is invoked as a warrior against the devil and all rebel angels. Prayer to St. Michael is especially powerful when we need deliverance from evil. For many years this traditional "St. Michael Prayer" was recited at the end of the Mass. Many, many Catholics retain it as part of their regular devotions:

St. Michael the Archangel, defend us in battle. Be our protection against the wickedness and snares of the devil. May God rebuke him, we humbly pray. And do thou, O prince of the heavenly host, by the power of God, cast into hell Satan and all other evil spirits who prowl about the world seeking the ruin of souls. Amen.

Ponder in Your Heart

Let us look for a moment at this appearance of angels in Jesus' life, for it will help us to better understand their role—their angelic mission—in all human life. Christian tradition describes the guardian angels as powerful friends, placed by God alongside each one of us, to accompany us on our way. And that is why he invites us to make friends with them and get them to help us . . .

We have to fill ourselves with courage, for the grace of God will not fail us. God will be at our side and will send his angels to be our traveling companions, our prudent advisers along the way, our cooperators in all that we take on. The angels "will hold you up with their hands lest you should chance to trip on a stone," as the psalm says.

We must learn to speak to the angels. Turn to them now . . . Ask them to take up to the Lord your good will, which, by the grace of God, has grown out of your wretchedness like a lily grown on a dunghill. Holy angels, our guardians: "defend us in battle so that we do not perish at the final judgment."

—St. Josemaría Escrivá, twentieth century

II

Life Times

6.

....

ADVENT AND CHRISTMAS

Christmas is a day and a season that requires no introduction, right? From the day after Halloween, the media and the storefronts relentlessly remind us of the holiday's imminence. The festival of Jesus' birth is the reason for the peak sales season in a retailer's year. Economists monitor it closely and analyze it endlessly as an indicator of the nation's financial health.

And I don't want to begrudge them a penny of it. Let the Grinches and Scrooges mutter darkly about the commercialization of Christmas. I'll take it (though not uncritically) as a tribute to Christ that society's great season of giving is the feast of his birth, even if that giving must be preceded by a season of buying.

I do, however, grieve for the eclipse of Advent; for the Church's season of spiritual preparation for Christmas has certainly been overwhelmed by the ever-expanding "Christmas shopping season." Advent is a season we must recover, even if it takes heroic effort.

In Advent the liturgy bids us to relive the period of expectation when the world awaited the Savior. We hear the words of the prophets, and we make them our own. The prophets longed for the conditions that Israel could only enjoy upon faithful fulfillment of the covenant. Instead, the people fell inexorably into sin, and so they lost the privileges God had given them: prosperity and happiness in a land flowing with milk and honey. The prophets ached for a messiah, ached for a redeemer, ached for a deliverer.

With the birth of Jesus came the fulfillment of all the holy desires of all those many centuries. That is the joy we mark in Christmas, but it's difficult for us to experience the joy unless we first undergo the longing.

That is why the Church leads us first through a season not of shopping, *but of longing.* Advent is sometimes called "the little Lent," because it is a season of preparatory fasting and self-denial. It is not as long as "Great Lent." In fact, it can be as short as twenty-one days. Yet it still should be a time of some small, daily sacrifices. The apostles fasted to prepare for worship in the Lord's presence (Acts 13:2). We should, too. That empty feeling should serve as a sensible sign of our spiritual need.

It is good for us, at least once a year, to recall the pain and poverty of a world without Christ. For centuries now, we have lived in a world shaped by Christian assumptions—Christian notions of right and wrong, of decency, of justice, and of human dignity. Now, as the world forgets Christ, all these natural benefits of his advent are vanishing as well. In post-Christian states, we have seen the notion of human dignity fade to non-existence, followed soon by human rights, beginning with the right to life. In a post-Christian world, we have seen ethnic minorities emerging anew—and violently—to wage brutal separatist wars against their closest cousins. The world is rapidly losing any sense of the transnational family Christ came to inaugurate, the kingdom where Israel and the Gentiles can live together in peace.

If we want to hold fast to the good things that came with Christ, then we must first keep a lively remembrance of the difference Christ made—the difference Christmas made. Advent calls us out of our cultural complacency. The Church echoes the prophets, who say: "Woe to those who are at ease in Zion" (Am 6:1), that is, those who have taken God's extraordinary gifts for granted.

If we are tempted to grumble about a culture that has forgotten Christ, then perhaps we are beginning to sense the longing of the prophets.

Christ has come, and yet we await him anew. He has saved us, and yet we still await a day when "he will wipe away every tear . . . and death shall be no more, neither shall there be mourning nor crying nor pain any more" (Rev 21:4). Christ has come, and he continues to come to us in the Eucharist. But he will come again, at the consummation of history. For this day, even the souls of the just in heaven cry out, "How long?" as did the ancient prophets (see Rev 6:10).

Advent reminds us that there are still two dimensions to our salvation: "already" and "not yet." In Advent we sing the ancient songs of longing and expectation, the "O Antiphons," because we await our Savior's coming in fullness, his "plenary parousia," as the theologians call it. When he comes at the end of time, he will have no more glory than he has now in the Eucharist, but then we'll see him as he is. The difference will be not with him, but with us: "we know that when he appears . . . we shall see him as he is" (1 Jn 3:2). Thus we hope for that day, and we fast through Advent, because, as we read in the very next line of St. John's letter: "everyone who thus hopes in him purifies himself as he is pure."

A blessed Advent, then, is the only true key to a merry Christmas. Christians should never be like the segments of affluent society that a social critic called "souls without longing." We should know longing habitually, because we have practiced longing at least annually, during Advent.

Advent is a time of vigilance, alertness, expectation. We are eager for the arrival of Christ, so we pay close attention to our life of prayer, our moral life, the way we treat others, and the way we express our love for God. We should not allow ourselves to experience "Xmas fatigue" long before December 25 rolls around. We should, if necessary, fast from the radio so that we don't hear an endless round of misplaced seasonal carols beginning the day after Thanksgiving, or fast from television programming that anticipates Christmas fulfillment during Advent's waiting. We should also show others that it is possible to buy for Christmas without bowing idolatrously to commercialism.

The Church is a refuge from a premature nativity. Catholic churches feel different during Advent (or they should). In the Mass, we eliminate the Gloria, because that is a Christmas song, the chant of the angels at the birth in Bethlehem (Lk 2:14). In fact, choirs and musicians are supposed to refrain from using *any* Christmas music during Advent liturgies.

Hope is the reason for the season, and Jesus Christ is certainly worth the wait. We could not reasonably expect a better Christmas present than Simeon and Anna received during that first octave of Christmas (Lk 2:25–38). They had waited long lives, not merely four weeks. Think, too, of the magi, who had scanned the skies in hope, looking for a sign.

We know him "already," but still "not yet." So let's keep our days as we should, looking for signs and then rejoicing in the mystery of the incarnation.

Ponder in Your Heart

Advent is celebrated for four weeks, to signify that this coming of the Lord is fourfold; namely, that he came to us in the flesh, that he came with mercy into our hearts, that he came to us in death, and that he will come to us again at the Last Judgment. The last week is seldom finished, to denote that the glory of the elect, as they will receive it at the last advent of the Lord, will have no end. But while the coming is in reality fourfold, the Church is especially concerned with two of its forms, namely with the coming in the flesh and with the coming at the Last Judgment. Thus the Advent fast is both a joyous fast, and a fast of penance. It is a joyous fast because it recalls the advent of the Lord in the flesh; and it is a fast of penance in anticipation of the advent of the Last Judgment.

With regard to the advent in the flesh, three things should be considered: its timeliness, its necessity, and its usefulness. Its timeliness is due first to the fact that man, condemned by his nature to an imperfect knowledge of God, had fallen into the worst errors of idolatry, and was forced to cry out, "Enlighten my eyes." Secondly, the Lord came in the "fullness of time," as St. Paul says in the Epistle to the Galatians. Thirdly, He came at a time when the whole world was ailing, as St. Augustine says: "The great physician came at a moment when the entire world lay like a great invalid." That is why the Church, in the seven antiphons that are sung before the Feast of the Nativity, recalls the variety of our ills and the timeliness of the divine remedy. Before the coming of God in the flesh, we were ignorant, subject to eternal punishment, slaves of the devil, shackled with sinful habits, lost in darkness, exiled from our true country. Hence the ancient antiphons announce Jesus in turn as our Teacher, our Redeemer, our Liberator, our Guide, our Enlightener, and our Savior.

As to the usefulness of Christ's coming, different authorities define it differently. Our Lord Himself, in the Gospel of Saint Luke, tells us that He came for seven reasons to console the poor, to heal the afflicted, to free the captives, to enlighten the ignorant, to pardon sinners, to redeem the human race, and to reward everyone according to his merits. And . . . St. Bernard says, "We suffer from a three-fold sickness: we are easily misled, weak in action, and feeble in resistance. Consequently the coming of the Lord is necessary, first to enlighten our blindness, second to succor our weakness, and third to shield our fragility."

—Jacobus de Voragine, thirteenth century

III

Stages of Life

7.

....

CONFIRMATION

Confirmation has been called a "sacrament in search of a theology," and a canonized saint has referred to the Holy Spirit as "the Great Unknown." Can it be that both our doctrine and our devotion are so impoverished—that we know neither the gift nor the giver?

May it never be so for you and me! For if we neglect the Holy Spirit and forget our confirmation, we are missing out on the very reason for our redemption. God became man not merely to save us *from* something (our sins), but to save us *for* something (to live as children of God). To be saved means nothing less than to share God's nature.

And so we do because of the gift of the Holy Spirit. Jesus told his apostles that the Spirit would "take what is mine and declare it to you" (Jn 6:14). It is the Spirit, then, who gives us our life in the Blessed Trinity. For it is the Spirit who gives us the life of the Son.

To send the Spirit was Jesus' stated purpose. He told his apostles: "It is to your advantage that I go away; for if I do not go away, the Counselor will not come to you; but if I go, I will send him to you . . . When the Spirit of truth comes, he will guide you into all the truth" (Jn 16:7, 13).

True to his promise, Jesus appeared to his apostles and "breathed on them, and said to them, 'Receive the Holy Spirit' " (Jn 20:22). Then, at the first Christian Pentecost, came a universal outpouring of the Holy Spirit upon the Church (Acts 2). This event had been foreshadowed in many Old Testament prophecies about the age of the Messiah (Is 44:3, 59:21; Ez 11:19, 36:25ff–27; Jl 2:28). Surely the greatness of the gift exceeded all expectation.

It was the gift not of something, but of Someone. It was the gift of the Holy Spirit.

It's clear from the Acts of the Apostles that Pentecost was an event intended for the entire Church, not just an elite, and not just for a day. It would be extended through time—institutionalized— by the sacraments. The gift of the Spirit came with baptism but was somehow completed by another rite. "Now when the apostles at Jerusalem heard that Samaria had received the word of God, they sent to them Peter and John, who came down and prayed for them that they might receive the Holy Spirit; for it had not yet fallen on any of them, but they had only been baptized in the name of the Lord Jesus. Then they laid their hands on them and they received the Holy Spirit" (Acts 8:14–17).

Tradition describes confirmation as the "seal" of the Holy Spirit. In the ancient world, to bear someone's seal, or wear it, was to be identified with that person, to be known as that person's child or servant. Confirmation marks us as God's own children. It con- fers a certain maturity upon us and empowers us to witness to the faith, defend the faith, and live responsibly within the Church. All these deeds are graces from God, and they do not depend upon our individual strengths or skills. The age at which a person is confirmed can vary widely from place to place. Some eastern churches confirm infants immediately after baptism, emphasizing the divine gratuity of the gift. Some western dioceses delay the sacrament until high-school matriculation or graduation, emphasizing that it is a sign of maturity, of coming into one's own in the Church. The Church teaches that confirmation, no matter when we receive it, "completes" our baptism.

We may wish to have received it at one age or another—earlier for the sake of the grace, or later for the sake of our understanding—but there's really no point to that. What we need to do is recognize that confirmation is a once-for-a-lifetime gift, and we can still call upon its grace every day of our lives. We have received all we need to reach spiritual maturity.

We receive what Christian tradition calls the "gifts of the Holy Spirit": wisdom, understanding, knowledge, counsel, piety, fortitude, and fear of the Lord. We also receive the fruits of the Holy Spirit, among them, for example: charity, joy, peace, patience, kindness, goodness, generosity, gentleness, faithfulness, modesty, self-control, and chastity.

When we see divisions in the Church—dissent, a lack of clarity, seemingly willful ignorance—then we see a need for the Holy Spirit. Rather than curse the darkness, we should invoke the third person.

We should examine ourselves on our devotion to the Holy Spirit and our appreciation for the day we were confirmed. Do we pray to the Holy Spirit as we pray to the Father and the Son? Do we pray to him personally? Because he is a person, not a force or an operation or an instrument.

If we are confirmed, then the Holy Spirit dwells within us. We are his temples (1 Cor 6:19). We don't have to go far to get to know him.

Christ came to earth in order to give us the Spirit. He ascended to the Father so that the Spirit could descend on the Church. In these divine actions, salvation history manifested the divine processions. The Father sending the Son in history is an image of the Father generating the Son in eternity. The descent of the Spirit upon the Church at Pentecost is an image of the Spirit's procession from the Father and the Son in eternity.

So we must strive not to neglect or undervalue the Spirit's life in the Trinity, or our life in the Spirit. The Spirit's essential work is to reproduce Christ's life, suffering, death, and resurrection in each and all of us. If we neglect the Spirit, then we are neglecting Christ, too.

Ponder in Your Heart

Now that you have been "baptized into Christ" and have "put on Christ," you have become conformed to the Son of God (Gal 3:27; Rom 8:29). For God "destined us to be his sons" (Eph 1:5) . . . Hence, since you "share in Christ" (Heb 3:14), it is right to call you Christs or anointed ones . . . You have become anointed ones by receiving the sign of the Holy Spirit. Since you are images of Christ, all the rites carried out over you have a symbolic meaning.

Christ bathed in the River Jordan, and having invested the waters with the divine presence of his body, he emerged from them, and the Holy Spirit visited him in substantial form, like coming to rest on like. In the same way, when you emerged from the pool of sacred waters you were anointed in a manner corresponding with Christ's anointing. That anointing is the Holy Spirit, of whom the blessed Isaiah spoke when he prophesied in the person of the Lord: "The Spirit of the Lord is upon me because he has anointed me" (Is 61:1) . . .

But be sure not to regard the [chrism] merely as ointment. Just as the bread of the Eucharist after the invocation of the Holy Spirit is no longer just bread, but the body of Christ, so the holy [chrism] after the invocation is no longer ordinary ointment but Christ's grace, which through the presence of the Holy Spirit instills his divinity into us.

—St. Cyril of Jerusalem, fourth century

8.

Marriage

I am not the first reader to note that the Bible is a book that tells a love story—the story of God's love for humankind. As if to emphasize the point, the Church arranged the Scriptures so that the biblical canon begins and ends with a wedding. In Genesis, the high point of the creation narrative is God's fashioning of man and woman, Adam and Eve, the primal two who become one flesh (Gen 2:23–24). In John's apocalypse, Revelation, the culmination is at the very end, in the seer's vision of heaven, which his angel guide describes as "the marriage supper of the Lamb" (Rev 19:9)—the celebration of the communion of Christ and his Church.

In between those two events, a love story unfolds. When God spoke through the prophets, he portrayed his covenant with Israel as a marriage. He spoke of himself, or his Messiah, coming as a bridegroom to take his people as his bride (see Hos 2:16–24; Jer 2:2; Is 54:4–8). Human marriage, then, was for Israel an earthly image of God's eternal love.

Some people wrongly caricature Israelite religion as "legalistic," simply because of its emphasis on the Law. But as Jon Levenson, a contemporary Jewish scholar, makes clear, "It is not a question of law *or* love, but law conceived in love, love expressed in law. The two are a unity." He goes on to explain that the Hebrew Scriptures are incomprehensible apart from this nuptial key: "What happened on the mountain in the ancient days was the consummation of a romance, a marriage in which YHWH was the groom and Israel . . . was the bride." Marriage got to the very meaning of the bond between God and his chosen people. It was a *covenant*—in Hebrew, *b'rith*—a family bond.

The joy, however, was not only for Israel. For all creation is caught up in the celebration of this "wedding" of heaven and earth. Through the prophet Hosea, God promises: "I will make for you a covenant on that day with the beasts of the field, the birds of the air, and the creeping things of the ground; and I will abolish the bow, the sword, and war from the land; and I will make you lie down in safety. And I will betroth you to me for ever; I will betroth you to me in righteousness and in justice, in steadfast love, and in mercy. I will betroth you to me in faithfulness; and you shall know the Lord" (2:18–20). Levenson concludes: "In the last stanza of Hosea's prophecy (vv. 23–25), all creation joins in the wedding ceremony. Sky responds to earth, and earth responds by bringing forth her bounty . . . The entire universe takes part in the sacred remarriage of YHWH and Israel."

Rabbi Michael Fishbane traces the influence of marital imagery from Hosea to Jeremiah (see Jer 2:2, 3:1). But, above all, he writes: "The topic of covenantal love between God and Israel came to celebrated expression in the classical rabbinic interpretations of the Song of Songs." Which tradition, a Christian might add, is found in the continuation of the Church's saints and scholars, from St.

Hippolytus and St. Gregory of Nyssa through St. Bernard of Clairvaux and St. Thomas Aquinas to Pope John Paul II.

The prophets foretold a new and everlasting covenant, which would be a renewal of the original covenant between God and Adam, God and humankind, God and all creation. It would, in fact, be so all encompassing as to be a "new creation." The imagery of the prophets, which was employed in turn by Jesus Christ, was the imagery of betrothal and marriage. Thus, when Jesus came, he called himself the "bridegroom" and those who were united to him in baptism were called "espoused" (see Jn 3:29; Mk 2:19; Mt 22:1–14, 25:1–13; 1 Cor 6:15–17; 2 Cor 11:2).

It is Jesus who gave us the first explicitly marital interpretation of Genesis. The word "marriage," after all, does not appear in the story of Adam and Eve. Yet, we know the story is about marriage because Jesus said it was (see Mk 10:2–16). Jesus said that the Genesis story reflects God's will "from the beginning of creation" and that "what God has joined together, no human being must separate."

Further along in the New Testament, St. Paul provided a profound mystical commentary. In his Letter to the Ephesians, he quoted the Genesis text and explained that this marriage covenant in the Garden is a reference to the covenant between "Christ and the Church" (see Eph 5:21–33). In using this unquestionable allusion to Adam and Eve becoming one flesh, Paul seems also to be shedding light on Adam's task and failure. He helps us see that Adam did *not* "give himself up" for his bride as he should have; instead, he allowed himself to be intimidated by the serpent. St. Paul helps us to see that Christ, on the other hand, does indeed "give himself up" for his bride, the Church. Where the first Adam had failed, with dire consequences, the new Adam succeeded, with saving power.

Note that Paul does not cancel out the literal meaning of the Genesis text, nor does he say it is not *truly* about real-world husbands and wives. In fact, he gives a beautiful teaching on the love that husbands and wives share. He is telling us, however, that marriage is also a symbol of a far greater mystery—the love that Christ has for his bride, the Church, the love that God has for his people.

This mystery receives its most powerful expression in the last book of the Bible, the Revelation of St. John, otherwise known as the Apocalypse—from the Greek word *apokalypsis,* which literally means "unveiling." Like the story of Adam and Eve, the Apocalypse evokes images that are both nuptial and priestly. Veils were then, as now, a standard part of a bride's wardrobe. The bride's "unveiling" was the culmination of the Jews' traditional weeklong wedding feast. Indeed, *apokalypsis* became associated with the first moment of marital intimacy and bodily communion, the physical consummation of the nuptial covenant.

Like a bride, God's sanctuary was veiled, to be unveiled only with the consummation of the New Covenant (see Mk 15:38). The holy of holies in Jerusalem's Temple was a four-square room, overlaid with gold (1 Kgs 6:19–20). It was shielded from sight by a floor-to-ceiling veil, a curtain embroidered with animal and floral decorations. (Thus, nature itself appeared as the symbolic "veil" of an even greater reality.) Yet the veil was torn, literally and symbolically, when Christ's body was torn in his act of self-giving love on the cross. Because of his self-offering, "we have confidence to enter the sanctuary by the blood of Jesus, by the new and living way which he opened for us through the veil, that is, through his flesh" (Heb 10:19–20).

That which is veiled is holy, to be unveiled only in covenant love. What the Apocalypse "unveils" is history's final consummation, the marriage of Christ to his bride, the Church (see Rev 19:9,

21:9, 22:17). She is "the holy city, New Jerusalem, coming down out of heaven from God, prepared as a bride adorned for her husband" (Rev 21:2). Like the holy of holies, Christ's bride is four-square and resplendent with pure gold (Rev 21:16–18).

By "unveiling" the Church, our priestly Bridegroom reveals the gift of his love to his bride—the New Jerusalem—in the "glory and beauty" of the Spirit (see Ex 28:2). The marriage inaugurates a new creation—"a new heaven and a new earth" (Rev 21:1).

It is a reprise of the opening chapters of Genesis. The third-century scholar Origen held that John's Apocalypse was the interpretive key to John's Gospel. Indeed, many puzzling aspects of the wedding feast at Cana seem to clear up when we understand that John is describing a new Genesis, a new creation, an eschatological "wedding feast" of the Lamb of God.

In the first covenant, we saw the marriage union of a man and a woman, Adam and Eve (see Gen 2:23–24). In the New Covenant, we see a new man and a new woman present at a wedding feast. True, Mary is Jesus' mother, not his bride. But in order to understand the supernatural depths of biblical symbolism that John intends here, we need to set aside our "natural" ways of reading. As the "woman," Mary becomes the locus of a host of biblical symbols and expectations. She is simultaneously a daughter of Israel, the mother of the new people of God, and the bride of God.

At Cana, Jesus appears as a New Adam, the firstborn of a new creation. What John implies is made clear elsewhere in the New Testament. Paul calls Jesus a "type" of Adam (see Rom 5:14) and the new or last Adam (see I Cor 15:21–22, 45–49). At Cana, Mary is the New Eve, the bride of the New Adam, the mother of the new creation.

At Cana comes the changing of water into wine—a transubstantiation that foreshadows Jesus' New Covenant meal: the Eucharist, the bodily consummation of the covenant between God and his Church. It is in the Eucharist that Jesus gives us his Body as food (Jn 6:26–58), and we, God's children, "share in flesh and blood" (Heb 2:14). It is in the Eucharist that Jesus draws all humanity to the marriage supper of the Lamb. It is in the Eucharist that Christ can look upon the Church as Adam looked upon Eve and say, "This at last is bone of my bones and flesh of my flesh" (Gen 2:23).

In the Eucharist we are made members of the wedding, each of us seated at the head table of the "marriage feast" that Jesus called "my banquet" in his parables. In the Eucharist, we enter into the depths of the communion of love that God intends for each person. In baptism, each of us is "betrothed to Christ" (2 Cor 11:2). Every Eucharist is our nuptial feast. "Every celebration," Augustine said, "is a celebration of marriage—the Church's nuptials are celebrated. The King's Son is about to marry a wife and . . . the guests frequenting the marriage are themselves the Bride . . . For all the Church is Christ's bride."

It is true of the Temple, and it is true of the bride. The connection is eminently clear in Jesus' mother tongue. The Hebrew word for holiness is *kiddushin,* which is also the word used for the Jewish wedding ceremony and for the state of matrimony.

When I first saw my beloved Kimberly on our wedding day, her beauty, even veiled, nearly knocked me off my feet. It was something mysterious, so much more than I could have expected. That wedding was a revelation to me. Little did I know that it was only a beginning, a genesis, a new creation, a new covenant.

Ponder in Your Heart

Marriage has God for its Author, and was from the very beginning a kind of foreshadowing of the incarnation of his Son; and therefore there abides in it something holy and religious; not extraneous, but innate; not derived from men, but implanted by nature.

—Pope Leo XIII, nineteenth century

9.

....

PRIESTHOOD

Before I was Catholic, I was anti-Catholic. As a high-school student I was active in para-church organizations that trained members to point out biblical "objections" to the Catholic faith. I often confronted Catholics with the words of Jesus: "call no man your father on earth" (Mt 23:9). Why then, I would ask, do Catholics address their priests as "Father"? I cringe now, not so much at my misunderstanding of Catholicism as my misunderstanding of the Bible.

After years of researching and praying, it became clear to me that the Scriptures indeed present God's priests as fathers. In biblical religion, a priest *is* a father—and even more a father than the man you or I might already call by that name "on earth," our natural or adoptive dads.

Let's begin at the beginning. In studying the Old Testament, we can divide the history of the priesthood into two periods: the patriarchal and the Levitical. The patriarchal period corresponds to the book of Genesis, while the Levitical period begins in Exodus and lasts until the coming of Jesus.

The religion of the patriarchal period was significantly different from the religion practiced by Israel after Moses received the Law on Mount Sinai. Patriarchal religion was firmly based on the natural family order, most especially the authority handed down from father to son—ideally the firstborn—often in the form of the "blessing" (see Gen 27).

In the book of Genesis, we find no separate priestly institution or caste. There is no temple set aside as the exclusive site of sacrifice. The patriarchs themselves build altars and present offerings at places and times of their own choosing (see Gen 4:3–4, 8:20–21, and 12:7–8). Fathers are empowered as priests by nature.

There are vestments associated with the office. When Rebekah took the garments of Esau, her firstborn, and gave them to Jacob (Gen 27:15), she was symbolically transferring the priestly office. We see the same priestly significance, a generation later, in the "long robe" that Jacob gave to his son Joseph (see Gen 37:3–4), and we understand why Joseph's half brothers were filled with envy.

Fatherhood is the original basis of priesthood. The very meaning of priesthood goes back to the father in the family—his representative role, spiritual authority, and religious service. The firstborn is the father's heir apparent, the one groomed to succeed one day to paternal authority and priesthood within the family. From the beginning, priesthood belonged to fathers and their "blessed" sons.

The pattern continued into the book of Exodus. There God declared to Moses, "Israel is my firstborn son" (Ex 4:22)—that is, among the many peoples of the earth, Israel was God's heir and his priest. At the Passover, the nation's firstborn sons were redeemed by the blood of the Paschal Lamb, and so they were consecrated to serve as priests within each of the twelve tribes and families of Israel (Ex 19:22–24). God gave Israel a unique vocation to be a "holy nation and a royal priesthood"—an "elder brother" in the family of nations. As the firstborn sons were to be priests in the family, so Israel was to act as God's firstborn son among the nations.

Still, there was a catch. Israel's status depended upon the biggest "if" in history: "if you obey my voice and keep my covenant" (Ex 19:5–6). In this, Israel failed. When the people worshiped the golden calf, the tribes of Israel forfeited the blessing of priesthood to one tribe, the Levites (Ex 32:25–29). For only the Levites resisted the temptation to idolatry.

Israel's priesthood thus became a hereditary office reserved to a cultural elite, and the home was no longer the primary place of priesthood and sacrifice. God had essentially "defrocked" the other tribes because of their infidelity. The Levites alone retained exclusive hold on Israel's priesthood through all the succeeding centuries, until the time of Jesus.

Even so, we can see in the book of Judges that Israel still identified priesthood with fatherhood. In the seventeenth chapter, we learn of a man named Micah, who consecrates his son a priest for the purpose of worship in the family's domestic shrine.

Yet, when a Levite appears at Micah's door, Micah pleads, "Stay with me, and be to me a father and a priest" (Jgs 17:10). A chapter later, Micah's plea is echoed, almost verbatim, by the Danites as they invite the Levite to be priest for their entire tribe: "Come with us, and be to us a father and a priest" (Jgs 18:19).

What's most remarkable about those requests is not what they assert, but what they assume. In just a few words, Micah provides us a rare glimpse of a transitional period for the people of Israel. Fathers were still installing their sons as priests in the domestic sanctuary—a custom left over from an earlier age. Yet the Levite's priesthood was already preferred to that of Micah's son—a hint of the newly emerging sacred order.

In the statement of Micah, and its repetition by the Danites, we also see that fatherhood was still considered an essential attribute of priestly ministry—even after priesthood had passed out of the family structure.

Those snippets from Judges are revealing. How embedded in the history of our religion—going back to its Israelite roots!—is this overarching reality of the spiritual paternity of the priest.

In the fullness of time, God the Father sent Jesus as a faithful firstborn son (Heb 1:6) and a priest (Heb 10:21)—not only to restore the natural priesthood, but also to establish a supernatural priesthood within the divine family, the Church.

Thus, with Jesus came a restoration of the natural priesthood of fathers and the establishment of a fatherly order of New Covenant priests. According to the Epistle to the Hebrews, Jesus' role and identity as the faithful firstborn Son of God (see Heb 1:6) qualify him as the perfect mediator between God, his Father, and us, his brothers and sisters. To Christ, we are "the children God has given me" (Heb 2:13), the "many sons" (Heb 2:10), "his brethren" (Heb 2:12), the new "seed of Abraham" (Heb 2:16), who together form God's "family/household," which Jesus builds and rules (Heb 3:3) as a son (Heb 3:6). As all Christians are identified with Christ, the Church becomes the "assembly of the firstborn" (Heb 12:23).

St. Peter, speaking to the Church, takes up the standard that Israel had lost in the desert: "You are a chosen race, a royal priesthood, a holy nation, God's own people" (1 Pet 2:9).

Now, once again, priests are fathers in the Church, which has now become "the universal family of God" (see CCC, nn. 1 and 1655). The apostles, who were Christ's first priests, clearly saw their own role as paternal. St. Paul asserts his spiritual fatherhood: "For though you have countless guides in Christ, you do not have many fathers. For I became your father in Christ Jesus through the gospel" (I Cor 4:15; see also Phil 2:22; I Tim I:2, I:18; 2 Tim I:2; Tit I:4; Phlm 10). Paul was a father not because he was married and reared a family; he did not. He was a father because he was a priest: "a minister . . . in the priestly service of the gospel" (Rom 15:16).

St. Augustine looked the same way upon the episcopal office he had inherited from the apostles: "The apostles were sent as fathers; to replace those apostles, sons were born to you who were constituted bishops . . . The Church calls them fathers, she who gave birth to them, who placed them in the sees of their fathers . . . Such is the Catholic Church. She has given birth to sons who, through all the earth, continue the work of her first Fathers."

That is the true biblical teaching. Our priests are so much more than managers or functionaries. They are fathers. The sacramental priesthood is not so much a ceremonial function as it is a family relation.

Thus, my pastor is father to a large family. Before God, he must take responsibility for thousands of people. His fatherhood is not merely metaphorical. True fatherhood involves the communication of life. As a natural father, I have communicated biological human life—but, in the sacraments of baptism and Eucharist, a priest communicates *divine life* and the *divine humanity* of Jesus Christ.

Because of his spiritual fatherhood, an ordained priest requires our respect—*every* priest, in spite of his weaknesses or sins. When God said, "Honor your father and your mother," he didn't qualify the commandment. He gave no exceptions. When a man fails in priesthood, we should pray for him, confront him privately with our concerns, confront him with other witnesses; and, if all other attempts fail, we should take our case to the bishop, all the while honoring the man, his priesthood, and his fatherhood. This is what children do for their fathers (see Gen 9:22–27).

Ponder in Your Heart

The reason that God—loving men of old—had for begetting children is no longer cited because the begetting of children no longer has this meaning for us, since we can observe with our own eyes how, by the help of God, thousands of nations and peoples from cities, lands, and fields come and gather through the evangelical teaching of our Redeemer, to attend together the divine instruction through the evangelical teaching. It is appropriate for the teachers and heralds of the true worship of God that they are now free of all the chains of earning a living and daily cares. Indeed, for these men it is now commanded to distance themselves resolutely from marriage so as to devote themselves to a more important matter. Now they are concerned with a holy and not a carnal begetting of descendants. And they have taken upon themselves the begetting, the God-pleasing education, and the daily care, not only of one or two children, but of an indeterminable number all at once.

—Eusebius of Caesarea, fourth century

10.

....

ANOINTING OF THE SICK

When Jesus commissioned the Twelve, they went out into the world and saw immediate results. In St. Mark's Gospel we learn that they "anointed with oil many that were sick and healed them" (Mk 6:13). They must have been astonished at the power flowing through them. Yet it was a mere shadow of the task that still lay ahead for them. For, as Jesus made clear elsewhere in St. Mark's Gospel, it is a greater work to forgive sins than to heal even the gravely ill (Mk 2:9).

Jesus healed people with dire illnesses and disabilities as a sign of spiritual healing: "that you may know that the Son of man has authority on earth to forgive sin" (Mk 2:10). The physical signs were there for the sake of a spiritual reality. They were a concession to human weakness.

In fact, after the apostles had witnessed many such marvels, Jesus assured them that they would accomplish "greater works than these" (Jn 14:12).

In the beginning of their ministry, the apostles, like Jesus, restored bodily health. But it was a sign of the deeper healing they would accomplish, through the Church, after Pentecost.

We catch a glimpse of the Church's ministry of spiritual healing in the Letter of St. James: "Is any among you sick? Let him call for the elders [presbyters, or priests] of the Church, and let them pray over him, anointing him with oil in the name of the Lord; and the prayer of faith will save the sick man, and the Lord will raise him up; and if he has committed sins, he will be forgiven" (Jas 5:14–15).

This is the sacrament we know today as the anointing of the sick.

But it's fair for us to ask why *physical* illness should be an occasion for a *spiritual* healing. There are many good reasons, not least that grave physical suffering is often accompanied by difficult spiritual trial. When we are in extremis, we are far more likely to be tempted to doubt God's goodness and power—or even his existence. Job's wife sincerely expected her husband to give in to despair and "curse God" (Jb 2:9).

Sacramental anointing gives us the grace we need to face such trials. Consider what the symbol of oil suggested to the early Christians. Oil healed, and oil strengthened. It was a base for many medicines. It was also a liniment used by athletes in the arena. Olive oil was the rubdown that strengthened wrestlers for a contest and enabled them to slip away from the grip of their enemies.

All of these worldly values are symbolic of the anointing's spiritual value for Christians. It heals us spiritually, and it strengthens us spiritually, to slip away from the devil's grasp and endure our contest with him—and, more than endure, to prevail, to be "more than conquerors through him who loved us" (Rom 8:37). The anointing even brings about that great marvel that Jesus alluded to in St. Mark's Gospel: the forgiveness of sins. Thus we can face even certain death with a serene mind and peaceful conscience, in the reasonable hope that death will be our gateway to eternal life.

Sometimes, the sacramental anointing will bring about a physical healing as well, if healing will be conducive to the salvation of the soul. That's wonderful, but unusual; and actually, it's far less a marvel than the sacrament's ordinary effects. Anointing is far more likely to give us what we really need: humble acceptance of our suffering, in union with the suffering of Christ and in atonement for sins, especially our own. Anointing helps us transform physical suffering into something more deeply remedial, something truly redemptive.

This was Christ's great gift to his suffering people: a more perfect share in his life. The early Church recognized the gift and showed tremendous gratitude. We find the sacrament extolled among the Syriac-speaking Christians by their great pioneer, St. Aphrahat. We find it praised in Egypt by St. Serapion, the companion of St. Athanasius. We find Pope Innocent I giving the Roman clergy detailed instructions for administering the sacrament.

Jesus came to bring *salvation*, a word that, in the ancient languages, is synonymous with "health." His physical cures were outward signs of a deeper and more lasting spiritual healing. Presumably, all the people he cured during his ministry died of normal causes. Presumably, then, their physical cure was of secondary importance, subordinate to an enduring healing, a spiritual healing, that would survive even the death of the body.

Though his healings were primarily spiritual, Jesus still worked them by physical means—for example, by smearing a man with mud and spittle (Jn 9:6–7). Why would God manifest his power by such humble, earthy means? He made us, and so he knows that we human beings learn through sensible signs and sacraments.

Moreover, he intended his work not just for his small number of contacts in an obscure land, in the brief time of his ministry. He established the Church on earth so that he could extend his incarnation—his healing, his salvation—through time and space.

Ponder in Your Heart

The Old and the New Testament give an important place to sickness and its healing, teaching us to see the relationship of both to the economy of salvation. Sickness is connected with sin and the devil; when God heals bodies, it is to care for souls as well; healing the sick, together with freeing those possessed by demons, is one of the signs of the reign of the Messiah.

It is by sin that sickness came into the world, with the pain of drudgery, the sufferings of childbirth, and death (Gen 3:15–19). Although sickness is not expressly mentioned in the curse of Adam and Eve, theological tradition has always rightly seen it as included . . .

Though Christ healed the sick and gave his Church power over disease, he did not abolish sickness. Neither has he abolished death, pain, or drudgery. However, like death, sickness has been conquered; the messianic era has been established once and for all. In the heavenly Jerusalem these ills will have no place; here below they still exist. But Christ has overcome sin and Satan, the cause of sin. Sickness has therefore lost its quality of being a curse. It can become redemptive, enabling the Christian to become like Christ in his passion and at the same time to witness to the power of the risen Christ in him. When Paul begged to be delivered from the sting that attacked his body, the Lord answered:

"My strength will find scope in your weakness" (2 Cor 12:9). In his own flesh Paul is to accomplish for the Church "what is lacking to the sufferings of Christ" (Col 1:24). "We bear at all times in our body the sufferings of the death of Jesus, that the life of Jesus also may be manifested in our body" (2 Cor 4:10).

—Aimé Georges Martimort, twentieth century

IV

Spice of Life

11.

INCENSE

Catholicism is sometimes called the religion of "bells and smells." Our tradition engages the whole person. God created us as a unity of body and soul, and we return ourselves entirely to him in worship. We worship him in spirit and truth (Jn 4:24); and in our "spiritual worship" we "present our bodies" too "as a living sacrifice" (Rom 12:1). Thus, the Church's worship engages all that we are, including our bodily and spiritual senses. In the liturgy, we contemplate the Gospel, but that's not all. We hear it, see it, feel it, taste it, and smell it as well. We ring bells to herald the Lord's appearance. We burn fragrant incense before his altar.

I remember the first time I attended a Catholic liturgical event, a vespers service at a Byzantine seminary. My Calvinist background had not prepared me for the experience—the incense and icons, the prostrations and bows, the chant and the bells. All my senses were engaged. Afterward a seminarian asked me, "What do you think?" All I could say was "Now I know why God gave me a body: to worship the Lord with his people in liturgy."

Our worship is not merely good and true. It is beautiful. We make it beautiful because it is for God. A generation or two ago, incense was used much more commonly in the Mass. I am not the first convert to confess that he was enchanted by his initial experience of incense. It was a pleasant experience, an aesthetic experience. There is good reason why non-Catholics came to associate us with bells and smells. They make a powerful impression.

So powerful, in fact, that some people worried whether incense was a distraction from true worship. They worried that it might reduce liturgy to a merely aesthetic experience, a religion of externals rather than true interior life. God had warned the Israelites against such pomp; and, through the prophet Isaiah, he even went so far as to tell them: "Bring no more vain offerings; incense is an abomination to me" (Is 13:1).

Yet God was not abolishing external forms of worship. He wanted his people to cease neglecting their interior dispositions. In fact, through the prophet Malachi, he foretold a day when "from the rising of the sun to its setting . . . in every place incense is offered to my name, and a pure offering" (Mal 1:11).

Indeed, incense was an important part of biblical religion—and it remains so—because God himself took care to make it so. The offering of incense was an essential duty of the priests of the Old Covenant, and the ancient law took special care to prescribe its fragrances, vessels, and rites (see, for example, Exodus, chapter 30). Of the high priest Aaron, God said: "I chose him out of all the tribes of Israel to be my priest, to go up to my altar, to burn incense" (1 Sam 2:28).

And so the priests did, from the time of Moses to the time of Jesus, and beyond. Jesus' kinsman Zechariah was performing his priestly duty, burning incense in the Temple, when the angel

Gabriel appeared to him. It was apparently customary for a "whole multitude of the people" to pray nearby "at the hour of incense" every day (see Lk 1:9–11).

Incense became the most emblematic form of worship. Grains of incense, once dropped into a thurible with hot coals, rise heavenward as fragrant smoke. It's meant to be an outward sign of the inner mystery that is true prayer. "Let my prayer be counted as incense before you," said the Psalmist (Ps 141:2). The metaphor still worked for St. Paul (see Phil 4:18). A Jewish theologian of the first century, Philo of Alexandria, saw the freedom of the censer's smoke rising heavenward as a symbol of mankind's spiritual and rational qualities, fashioned after the divine image. When incense was offered with animal sacrifice, he said, it symbolized the entirety of human nature, body and soul, given to God.

So closely was incense associated with worship that, for the prophets, the very image of infidelity was to burn incense to idols. "I will utter my judgments against them, for all their wickedness in forsaking me; they have burned incense to other gods, and worshipped the works of their own hands" (Jer 1:16).

That image, too, worked just as well in the early centuries of Christianity, when Roman law required all citizens to burn incense before the emperor's protector deity. In offering the pinch of incense, some Christians saved their lives (temporarily), but committed the mortal sin of apostasy. They abandoned true worship for false; and, in doing so, they excommunicated themselves from the Church. The Christian who remained true referred to the traitors as "thurifers"—incense burners.

Thus, for all the ancients, to burn incense was to offer a richly symbolic act of worship. When St. John the Seer wanted words to depict the worship of the angels in heaven, he described it as attended by the rising smoke of much incense (see Rev 5:8). The prayers of the saints on earth, he says, rise as incense to heaven (see Rev 8:3–4).

Incense belongs with worship. It is not necessary, but it is beautiful and expressive, and worthy of divine worship. God prescribed it in the Law, not for *his* sake, but for ours, so that we might see, through this sign, the beauty of worship.

In the time of Jesus, incense was burned not only in the Temple, but also in the "communion" meal, the *chaburah* we discussed in chapter 4. The rabbis debated, at great length, the proper use of incense in this ritual of hearth and home.

How much more should we take care to incorporate this aromatic sign in the Mass—the meal of our New Covenant fellowship.

The earliest Christian documents—the *Didache*, St. Justin, St. Irenaeus—applied the prophecy of Malachi 1:11 to the Eucharist. The Holy Mass, they said, was the pure offering, the always-and-everywhere offering of incense to the God of Israel. St. Paul said it well: "But thanks be to God, who in Christ always leads us in triumph, and through us spreads the fragrance of the knowledge of him everywhere. For we are the aroma of Christ to God among those who are being saved . . . a fragrance from life to life" (2 Cor 2:14–16).

Ponder in Your Heart

Sovereign Lord Jesus Christ, O Word of God, who freely offered yourself a blameless sacrifice upon the cross to God the Father, the coal of double nature, that touched the lips of the prophet with the tongs and took away his sins: touch also the hearts of us sinners, and purify us from every stain, and present us holy beside your holy altar, that we may offer you a sacrifice of praise. Accept from us, your unprofitable servants, this incense as a sweet-smelling fragrance, make fragrant the evil odor of our soul and body, and purify us with the sanctifying power of your all-holy Spirit . . .

Accept from the hands of us sinners this incense, as you accepted the offering of Abel, and Noah, and Aaron, and Samuel, and of all your saints, guarding us from everything evil, and preserving us for continually pleasing, worshipping, and glorifying you . . .

We render thanks to you, the Savior and God of all, for all the good things you have given us, and for the communion of your holy and pure mysteries. We offer you this incense, praying: Keep us under the shadow of your wings, and count us worthy till our last breath to partake of your holy rites for the sanctification of our souls and bodies, for the inheritance of the kingdom of heaven. For you, O God, are our sanctification, and we send up praise and thanksgiving to You, Father, Son, and Holy Spirit.

—Prayers of Incense, from the Divine Liturgy of
St. James, fourth century or earlier

12.

··

CANDLES

When the people of Israel offered worship in the Old Testament, they did so amid the flicker of many lights. "So Solomon made . . . the lampstands of pure gold, five on the south side and five on the north, before the inner sanctuary" (I Kgs 7:48–49). So important were these candelabra that the main one, the Temple menorah, became the most recognizable symbol of Judaism. It appears on countless coins, amulets, and house lamps from antiquity. When the Roman emperor Titus wished to memorialize his conquest of Jerusalem, he did so with an image of his troops carrying away the menorah.

We have every indication that the apostles saw their Eucharist in continuity with the worship of the Temple. It presented itself, in fact, as the fulfillment of Temple worship. This is evident in the cultic language used by the Apostolic Fathers (e.g., *sacrifice, offering,* and *altar*); and it is recognized by Jewish as well as Christian biblical scholars. In his commentary on Leviticus, Baruch Levine wrote: "Christian worship in the form of the traditional mass affords the devout an experience of sacrifice, of communion, and proclaims that God is present. The Christian church, then, is a temple."

The generation of the apostles observed that continuity in many ways, employing in the liturgy many of the details formerly associated with Temple worship. This is evident in the New Testament treatment of lights and lamps.

In one of history's earliest descriptions of Christian liturgy, we find St. Paul preaching in a crowded room. St. Luke notes that "There were many lights in the upper chamber where we were gathered" (Acts 20:8). So many lights in such a small space would be tremendous overkill—unless they served ceremonial rather than utilitarian purposes.

When we arrive at the Apocalypse, at the close of the New Testament Scriptures, St. John shows us the worship of heaven in images that consistently reflect earthly worship. Everywhere there are lamp stands. The lights shine as a symbol of the life of the Church. If a Church is falling slack in its devotion, John warns that God could remove its lamp stand (see Rev 2:5). In a stunning liturgical image, Christ appears, vested as a priest, amid the light of many lamps (Rev 1:12–13). Surely, this was a familiar image—that of the Christian clergy who offered the liturgy "in the person of Christ" (*en prosopo Christou*, 2 Cor 2:10).

The lamp was itself a symbol of Jesus Christ, who consistently spoke of his Gospel and even of himself in terms of light. "I am the light of the world; he who follows me will not walk in darkness, but will have the light of life" (Jn 8:12). *Illumination* (sometimes rendered "enlightenment") was among the early Church's most common synonyms for baptism (see Heb 10:32). Still today, on the Church's great celebration of baptism, the Easter Vigil liturgy, the priest holds aloft the paschal candle and proclaims "Christ our light!" three times.

The lamp is a symbol of Christ, God's presence among us. Yet it is still more. Christ came not just to light our way, but to give us his light as our own. The God-man who revealed himself to be the light of the world also told his followers: "You are the light of the world" (Mt 5:14). So closely are Christians identified with Christ that we come, through illumination, to be lights ourselves. We are partakers of the divine light (2 Pt 1:4); by grace it becomes our nature, too! Thus we can truly sing: *This little light of mine, I'm gonna let it shine.*

The early Church Fathers attest to the abundant use of lights in Christian worship, far beyond mere functionality. The greatest Scripture scholar in the ancient world, St. Jerome, delighted in this custom of the Church: "whenever the Gospel is to be read the candles are lighted—although the dawn may be reddening the sky— *not of course to scatter the darkness, but by way of showing our joy.*"

Again, the candles represent the light of Christ, but it is a light he has shared with his chosen people, his saints. Jerome notes that Jesus described St. John the Baptist as "a burning and shining lamp" (Jn 5:35). Thus, Christians, even today, follow the example of Jesus as we light candles at the chapels of the saints. Jerome recalls the funeral of a holy woman, St. Paula, whose body was attended in procession by many bishops bearing lights. He also describes the numerous wicks that burned at the shrines of the martyrs. And still today, we burn candles at the shrines of the saints. We join our prayers with theirs.

St. Athanasius of Alexandria referred to the lighting of votive candles as an "offering" of the faithful. When many of them are alight—whether before an image of Jesus, or Mary, or the saints— it gives great glory to God, who has shared his glory with us. St. Paulinus of Nola described such a shrine in the late fourth century: "With crowded lamps are these bright altars crown'd, and waxen tapers shedding perfume round / from fragrant wicks, beam calm a scented ray / to gladden night, and joy e'en radiant day . . . countless lamps in never-ending blaze."

Said St. Jerome: "Under the figure of material light, that light is represented of which we read in the Psalter, 'Your word is a lamp unto my feet, O Lord, and a light unto my paths' (Ps 119:105)." That light is Christ. And by grace it is his saints, too. It's you, and it's me.

Let it shine, let it shine, let it shine!

Ponder in Your Heart

The lamps that you kindle are a sacrament of the illumination [of baptism] by means of which we shall meet the Bridegroom as shining and virgin souls, with the lamps of our faith shining, not sleeping through our carelessness, that we may not miss him that we look for if he come unexpectedly; nor yet unfed, and without oil, and destitute of good works, that we be not cast out of the bridal chamber [see Mt 25:1–13]. For I see how pitiable is such a case. He will come when the cry demands the meeting, and those who are prudent shall meet him, with their light shining and its food abundant.

—St. Gregory Nazianzen, fourth century

13.

···

SACRED IMAGES

A colossal mosaic, *Christ in Majesty*, dominates the great upper church at the Basilica Shrine of the Immaculate Conception in Washington, D.C. It is a fierce portrayal of Jesus, his passion restrained only by the fixity of the Byzantine style.

It's an image that resonates with me on many levels. Through my earliest years as a Christian—through my teens, through college and through seminary preparation for Presbyterian ministry—my formation was overwhelmingly Calvinist, a Protestant tradition that emphasizes God's sovereignty and his judgment. "For the Lord is our judge, the Lord is our ruler, the Lord is our king," said the prophet Isaiah (Is 33:22). And that's how Jesus appears in the Basilica. The irony is that my Calvinist background prepared me to think of Christ that way, but not to *see* him that way—at least not in this life. The reformer John Calvin was a forceful opponent of devotional images, favoring bare church walls and even bare crosses. He held that images—even images of Christ—presented a temptation to idolatry, the worship of a temporal sign in place of the sovereign and transcendent Lord.

I am now more than two decades a Roman Catholic. Yet every time I kneel beneath that overpowering image I wonder whether it is my vestigial inner Calvinist that thrills at such an expression of God's sovereignty—thrilling, nevertheless, as only a Catholic can thrill before a sacred image.

Some years ago, an essayist nicknamed this icon "Scary Jesus." And it is a little scary. It certainly seems to violate the canons of the Christian greeting-card industry. Contemporary Christian images bid us imagine the Lord backing up the goalie in a junior-varsity soccer game, or hugging teens on prom night. In modern images, Jesus often looks like a nice guy Norman Rockwell somehow missed in all those *Saturday Evening Post* covers. "Scary Jesus" doesn't fit the profile.

Still, there is a more disquieting paradox at work in *Christ in Majesty*. The mosaic portrays Christ in judgment, as we might encounter him in the book of Revelation. Yet doesn't the same book portray Christ as a lamb, so gentle that he can pass for dead (Rev 5:6)? Didn't the Word become flesh as a man who blessed the meek and didn't fight back?

The icon forces us to confront a seeming contradiction in Christianity: our Lord is a just judge, a powerful vindicator, whose wrath is capable of consigning mortal sinners to hell; yet our Lord is merciful and as meek as a lowly barnyard animal in its infancy.

Some people have tried to reconcile these images by making them sequential. Jesus was soft and tender in his first coming, they say, but with the second coming the gloves will be off, and then it's no more Mr. Nice Guy. Well, this doesn't work for several reasons: first, because the Gospels show us that Jesus did indeed vent his wrath on wicked men during his earthly life; but also because the book of Revelation shows our Lord to be a lamb to the very end, at the consummation of all human history.

So which shall we worship? Which shall we contemplate? The Judge or the Lamb? Scary Jesus or Mr. Nice Guy? Which is the true Lord and Christ?

The dogmatic truth is that we need not choose. The mystery of the incarnation demands that we accept the perfect union of many seemingly incompatible things: the finite contains the infinite; the eternal enters time; the sacrificial lamb presides on the Day of Wrath.

This is not a subtlety reserved for theologians. Dockworkers and poultry keepers, washer women and seamstresses have known this since the birthday of the Church. Even Christians who couldn't read knew the truth of Christ because of sacred images like *Christ in Majesty*.

In the eighth century a movement arose in the eastern churches to do away with religious images. It was a movement of elites—intellectuals, theologians, and emperors. They thought that icons were an insult to God's glory and majesty, which cannot really be portrayed. The transcendent God should be worshipped only with the intellect, they said. They received an imperial license to destroy the icons in the churches; and for this they earned the name *iconoclasts*, image smashers.

The saints, however, opposed these elites, and the saints prevailed. These holy men and women called themselves *iconodules*— "those who honor icons." They argued that since God had condescended to take on flesh, the common people had the right to contemplate him enfleshed. The most eloquent of the iconodules, St. Theodore of Studion, wrote that Christ "does not abandon the exalted reality of his divinity, which is immaterial and cannot be circumscribed; and yet it is his glory to abase himself in such a noble manner down to our own level that now in his body he can be circumscribed. He has become matter, that is: flesh, he who sustains everything that exists; and he is not ashamed to have become what he has taken on, and to be called such."

What the face of the human Jesus revealed during his life on earth during the first century, sacred images reveal nowadays. Even when a picture portrays Christ as a ruler and judge, it portrays him as a human being and reminds us of his humility, his willingness to join in the human condition, with all its weaknesses. Throughout history, some people have been scandalized by God's assuming human flesh in Jesus—by his bleeding and dying. They wanted him safely back in his heaven as purely divine. But that cannot be, because, as John's Gospel reminds us, the Word was made flesh and dwelt among us—and he still has that flesh. He didn't shed it the way a snake sheds its skin when he died. He glorified that flesh and now offers it as love to the Father. What is scandalous about these images is simply the scandal of the incarnation, with all its paradoxes.

Ponder in Your Heart

Since some find fault with us for worshipping and honoring the image of our Savior and that of Our Lady, and those, too, of the rest of the saints and servants of Christ, let them remember that in the beginning God created man after his own image (Gen 1:26). On what grounds, then, do we show reverence to each other unless because we are made after God's image? For as

Basil, that much-versed expounder of divine things, says, the honor given to the image passes over to the prototype . . . Why was it that the Mosaic people honored the tabernacle (Ex 33:10) that bore an image and type of heavenly things, or rather of the whole creation? God indeed said to Moses, "See that you make them after the pattern for them, which is being shown you on the mountain" (Ex 25:40). The Cherubim, too, which overshadow the mercy seat, are they not the work of men's hands (Ex 25:18)? What, further, is the celebrated Temple at Jerusalem? Is it not handmade and fashioned by the skill of men (1 Kgs 8)? . . .

God in the depths of his pity became true man for our salvation . . . he lived upon the earth and dwelt among men (Bar 3:38), worked miracles, suffered, was crucified, rose again and was taken back to heaven. Since all these things actually took place and were seen by men, they were written for the remembrance and instruction of us who were not alive at that time, so that though we saw not, we may still, hearing and believing, obtain the blessing of the Lord. But not every one can read; nor does everyone have time for reading. So the Fathers gave their approval to depicting these events on images . . . in order that they should form a concise memorial of them. Often, doubtless, when we do not have the Lord's passion in mind and see the image of Christ's crucifixion, his saving passion is brought back to memory, and we fall down and worship not the material but that which is depicted—just as we do not worship the material from which the Gospels are made, nor the material of the cross, but that which these symbolize . . . It is just the same in the case of the mother of the Lord. For the honor we give her is referred to him who was made flesh from her . . . The honor rendered to the image passes over to the prototype.

—St. John of Damascus, eighth century

14.

....

RELICS

So completely do the saints correspond to God's grace that—for a millennium and more after their bodies have lain lifeless—their very bones remain a channel of grace. Long before the coming of Christ, the prophet Ezekiel beheld a vision of a field of dry bones, and the Lord God said to the bones: "Behold, I will cause breath to enter you, and you shall live" (Ez 37:5). The Lord God breathed on the bones, and indeed they returned to life. Yet the breath of God accomplishes still more that that. It renders the bones of his chosen people not only *living*, but truly *life-giving*.

Consider another story from the age of the prophets. "And as a man was being buried, lo, a marauding band was seen and the man was cast into the grave of Elisha; and as soon as the man touched the bones of Elisha, he revived, and stood on his feet" (2 Kgs 13:21). By the mere touch of the prophet Elisha's lifeless bones, life returned to a dead man's body—so great is the grace of God as it works through the bodies of the saints. That principle was true in the Old Covenant as well as the New. The prophet Elisha understood it while he was still alive. Once, when he needed to cross a river, he simply struck the water with the garment of his master Elijah, and the waters parted before him (see 2 Kgs 2:14). By the time of Jesus, believers took the doctrine of relics for granted. In the Gospels we find a woman who "suffered from a hemorrhage for twelve years." Though she had given up on medical doctors, she knew she could trust in the touch of something that had touched the sacred. As Jesus passed by, she said to herself, "If I only touch his garment, I shall be made well" (Mt 9:20–21). And she was made well.

Before Jesus ascended to heaven, he breathed upon the Church (Jn 20:22) and imparted his life-giving Spirit. Thereby his healing ministry passed to the saints; and the New Testament shows them busy about it: "And more than ever believers were added to the Lord, multitudes both of men and women, so that they even carried out the sick into the streets, and laid them on beds and pallets, that as Peter came by at least his shadow might fall on some of them. The people also gathered from the towns around Jerusalem, bringing the sick and those afflicted with unclean spirits, and they were all healed" (Acts 5:14–16).

Decades passed, and still "God did extraordinary miracles by the hands of Paul, so that handkerchiefs or aprons were carried away from his body to the sick, and diseases left them and the evil spirits came out of them" (Acts 19:11–12).

All it took was the brush of an apostle's body, the touch of his hanky or apron—even just his shadow!

Is it any wonder that the early Christians continued to place great trust in the relics of the saints? Archaeologists have turned up ample evidence of this devotion, dating back to the deaths of

Saints Peter and Paul in Rome. The faithful took care to preserve their remains, and pilgrims streamed to the city to venerate them and touch them.

Nor did the Church reserve such veneration exclusively for the bones of the apostles. The early Christians built many churches over the graves of the martyrs. This was a decisive break with the traditions of the Romans and the Jews, who (like most ancient peoples) considered human corpses to be defiling and unclean— death-dealing rather than life-giving.

Yet Christians believed in the marvelous exchange: Christ became what we are so that we might become what he is. He came to divinize us, body and soul and flesh and bones and blood. So the bodies of the saints now convey his life to the world.

Christians celebrated that fact with great joy, great pomp, and great churches—St. Peter's Basilica, St. Paul's Outside the Walls: these are grand reliquary churches, built upon gravesites. The emperor Julian, who led the charge in the late fourth century to repaganize the Roman Empire, detested the Christians for their cult of relics: "you have filled the whole world with tombs and sepulchers," he said.

Inside the basilicas, the Church constructed its altars directly over the caskets of the apostles and martyrs. Over time, it became customary for all Catholic parishes to deposit small relics of the saints within a sealed cavity inside the church's altar. Thus, every Church on earth could follow, in a sensible way, after the spiritual worship St. John glimpsed in heaven: "When he opened the fifth seal, I saw under the altar the souls of those who had been slain for the word of God and for the witness they had borne" (Rev 6:9).

The Church's most precious relics, however, are those associated with Jesus' life and ministry, passion and death. Thus the whole of Christendom contributes for the care of the shrines in the Holy Land, where Jesus spent his earthly life. The Church of the Holy Sepulchre rises above Jesus' tomb, as the Church of the Nativity stands on the traditional site of his birth. Documents dating to the fourth century show the intensity of Christians' devotion to the wood of the true cross. In fact, sometimes people got carried away by their devotion. In ancient times, during Holy Week, the Bishop of Jerusalem would customarily call forth his congregation to kiss the relics of the true cross, and one year a man bit off a chunk before walking away!

So I'm emphatically *not* saying that the doctrine of relics was, always and everywhere, very clearly understood.

But as it was in the ancient Church, so it remains today: to venerate relics is something distinctly and characteristically Christian.

Ponder in Your Heart

[Addressed to a heretic, Vigilantius, who rejected the veneration of relics:]

Tell us more clearly—so that there may be no restraint on your blasphemy—what you mean by the phrase "a bit of powder wrapped up in a costly cloth in a tiny vessel."

It is nothing less than the relics of the martyrs that he is troubled to see covered with a costly veil, and not bound up with rags or hair-cloth, or thrown in the dump, so that Vigilantius alone in his drunken slumber may be worshipped.

Are we, therefore, guilty of sacrilege when we enter the basilicas of the apostles? Was the Emperor Constantius I guilty of sacrilege when he transferred the sacred relics of Andrew, Luke, and Timothy to Constantinople? In their presence the demons cry out (Acts 8:7, 5:16)—and the devils who dwell in Vigilantius confess that they feel the influence of the saints. And at the present day is the Emperor Arcadius guilty of sacrilege, who after so long a time has conveyed the bones of the blessed Samuel from Judea to Thrace? Are all the bishops to be considered not only sacrilegious, but silly into the bargain, because they carried that most worthless thing, dust and ashes, wrapped in silk in golden vessel? Are the people of all the churches fools, because they went to meet the sacred relics, and welcomed them with as much joy as if they beheld a living prophet in their midst, so that there was one great swarm of people from Palestine to Chalcedon with one voice re-echoing the praises of Christ? . . .

You show mistrust because you think only of the dead body, and therefore blaspheme. Read the Gospel: The God of Abraham, the God of Isaac, the God of Jacob: he is not the God of the dead, but of the living (Mt 22:32). If, then, they are alive, they are not, to use your expression, kept in honorable confinement.

—St. Jerome, fifth century

15.

....

FASTING AND
MORTIFICATION

You'll sometimes hear people say that fasting and bodily discipline are "outmoded" expressions of Catholic spirituality. But that's not true. As long as we follow Christ, we will have to deny our bodies the things they want. Jesus said: "If any man would come after me, let him deny himself and take up his cross and follow me" (Mt 16:24). St. Paul put it in stronger terms when he told the Colossians to "put to death therefore what is earthly in you" (Col 3:5).

All the things of the earth are good, because God has made them. Yet there's no doubt that our desire for many of them is out of whack. Given the opportunity, most of us will eat more than our bodies need, and that's not good for us. In fact, this may be worse for the soul than it is for the body. For we become attached to created things and to the pleasure they bring us. And in time, we prefer the pleasure to spiritual goods. We'd rather take a nap or watch a sitcom than pray the Rosary. We'd rather stay tuned to a talk radio host who amuses us, even though we know he tempts us to sin against charity when he belittles politicians. We eagerly take another beer, even though we know that our physician and our confessor are united in opposing this move.

St. Augustine said that sin begins as a turning away from God and a turning toward lesser goods. When we sin, we don't choose evil. We choose something less than God and his will.

Again, our bodies incline us this way. Ever since the sin of our first ancestors, our bodily appetites are disordered. So, as long as we have bodies, they will need to be disciplined. Our bodies want more than they need, so we must give them less than they want.

How do we do this? Our methods are not unlike the methods we use to obtain difficult earthly goals. If we want to get in shape, what do we do? We exercise. We diet. The harder we strive, the better the results. If we want to advance in our career, how do we go about it? We forgo pleasures and spend more time in concentrated work. Think of the slogans that drive us: "No pain, no gain." An accountant I know told me that the unofficial motto in his firm was: "Don't date—work late."

For earthly or heavenly goals, our bodies need discipline. Our bodies must be subject to our reason—or the order will be reversed: our reason will soon be subject to our bodies. The early Christians knew this, and they fasted frequently. St. Paul went even further: "I pommel my body and subdue it" (1 Cor 9:27).

When we fast, we follow consistent biblical models. Moses and Elijah fasted before going into God's presence (Ex 34:28; 1 Kgs 19:8). Anna the prophetess fasted to prepare herself for the coming of the Messiah (Lk 2:37). Jesus fasted (Mt 4:2), even though he needed no purification. So he must have done this for the sake of our imitation. In fact, he assumed that we would follow his example. "When you fast," he said, "do not look gloomy like the hypocrites" (Mt 6:16). He did not say "*if* you fast," but "when."

The Church requires certain disciplines of us. We must fast for an hour before receiving Holy Communion. It's a small sacrifice, and it may even produce a "sacramental hunger" in us—not only a hunger for the sacrament, but a hunger that is itself a bodily sign of a spiritual reality: our desire for union with the Lord. Surely that's why the apostles fasted in preparation for the liturgy (see Acts 13:2–3).

We are required to make substantial fasts on two days every year, Ash Wednesday and Good Friday. On those days, we may take only one full meal, and that meal must not be greater than the other meals combined. On those two days, and on all the Fridays of Lent, we may not eat meat. (Actually, the Church suggests that we abstain from meat on all the Fridays of the year, or substitute some other sacrifice.)

Measured against the sacrifices we've made in other areas of life—school, work, parenting, even sports—these don't add up to much. But our faithfulness in these small renunciations should be an indicator of our constant fidelity to that daily self-denial that Jesus demands from us. We should make a habit of it, and give special preference to those sacrifices that make others happy: choosing the movie my spouse would rather see, or leaving the last portions of a snack for my children to enjoy.

By voluntary self-denial, we return to God what is his; and we demonstrate our preference for spiritual goods. In due course, we will lose the good things one by one. How much better for us if we give them up voluntarily, for love? If our self-denial is habitual, then perhaps we won't grow so bitter when age takes away our delights, as it certainly will, without asking our permission. The Catholic author Jorge Luis Borges wrote a story that symbolically depicted the limits of sensory pleasure. The narrator, an old man, dreams that our enjoyment of earthly pleasures is limited by a fated number: "You will use up the number that corresponds to ginger and you will go on living. You will use up the number that corresponds to the smoothness of crystal and you will go on living a few more days."

We will all face death someday. Some people face it with serenity and even joy, in expectation of fulfillment and gain. Others face it in misery because of their losses.

If all life is a preparation for the moment of death, Jesus' advice on daily self-denial indeed makes good sense. "So you have sorrow now, but I will see you again and your hearts will rejoice, and no one will take your joy from you" (Jn 16:22).

"When you fast," Jesus said, "do not look gloomy." And we who fast do have every reason to rejoice. When we live this way, we imitate Christ, who enjoyed perfect freedom because no one could take anything away from him. He had already voluntarily given up even himself (Jn 10:17).

Imitating him would be enough. But we do still more. We share his life and his divine work of redemption. We can apply the fruits of our self-denial to others, as an act of love. Like St. Paul, we can say: "Now I rejoice in my sufferings for your sake, and in my flesh I complete what is lacking in Christ's afflictions for the sake of his body, that is, the Church" (Col 1:24).

Ponder in Your Heart

Let us fall to fasting, to prayer, to almsgiving in time and give that unto God that may be taken from us. If the devil put in our mind the saving of our land and our goods, let us remember that we cannot save them long. If he fear us with exile and fleeing from our country, let us remember that we be born into the broad world, and not like a tree to stick in one place, and that whithersoever we go, God shall go with us.

—St. Thomas More, sixteenth century

V

Abundant Life

16.

CONFESSION

Confession is the way God's people have always gone about repenting, healing, and reconciling. Read the first pages of the Bible, and you'll find God asking Adam, "Where are you?" Later, God asks the murderer Cain, "Where is your brother?" The Almighty isn't looking for information. He already knows everything. He's looking for the one thing Adam or Cain should have given him, but didn't—and that's a full confession. He wanted it for their sake, so that they might live again in the truth. Unfortunately, it was not forthcoming.

Go through the rest of the Old Testament, however, and you'll find that God taught the people of Israel many ways to confess their sins and make amends—with sacrifices, sin offerings, and burnt offerings. It was hard work, expensive and bloody. A penitent had to buy his own animal, bring it to the altar, and slaughter it himself. But he could walk away with a certain peace of mind, having made his confession and completed the penance that God required.

The human need for confession didn't vanish with the coming of Jesus. But now it's fulfilled in a neater, easier, and more powerful way. Jesus responded to it perfectly, by establishing a ministry and a sacrament of penance in the Church.

There are many ways of looking at confession, and all of them are valid. You can look at it as a courtroom with a divine judge. You can look at it as an accounting of debts. I think it's most helpful to look at it as healing—as health care. Confession does for our souls what doctors, dieticians, physical therapists, and pharmacists do for our bodies.

Think about all we do to keep our bodies in working order. We go for regular checkups with a primary-care physician, a dentist, an eye doctor. And no one has to remind us to brush our teeth, take a shower, and pop the pills for whatever ails us. All this is good for us, and it's good for everyone around us, too. No one wants to work beside us if we decide to stop showering.

Well, if we spend so much effort on the care of our bodies, shouldn't we be spending more time on our souls? After all, our bodies will pass away soon enough, but our souls will live on forever.

What's more, our decisions about our spiritual health and hygiene will have a *tremendous* effect on the people around us. Nothing serves family life and workplace dynamics so well as a clean soul and the advice of a good confessor. On the other hand, nothing hurts our relationships and our mental health so much as the burden of sin and guilt. Confession is free health care, and free life insurance as well! Christ is the divine physician; and, unlike human physicians, he can guarantee us a cure every time. In fact, he can guarantee us immortality. Any doctor who could do all that would have long lines stretching from his office door. The thing that will make confession less intimidating is a stronger faith in Jesus Christ and what he can do for us.

When your body's hurting, you need to see a doctor. You might not *want* to see a doctor. You might not find doctor visits particularly pleasant. Maybe you even have a deep-seated fear of doctors' offices. But nothing else will do to set your broken limb, purge your body of a bug, or close up your bleeding wound. It won't help you to visit your accountant or your auto mechanic.

The New Testament rite differs from the Old because now God himself serves as high priest. The scribes and pharisees were right when they asked Jesus, "Who can forgive sins but God alone?" (Mk 2:7). What they would not believe was that Jesus is the Son of God. Only Jesus could say with authority: "My son, your sins are forgiven" (Mk 2:5).

Jesus had the authority to share that power with his chosen clergy, his apostles. And that's precisely what he did, on the day of his resurrection: "He breathed on them, and said to them, 'Receive the Holy Spirit. If you forgive the sins of any, they are forgiven; if you retain the sins of any, they are retained'" (Jn 20:22–23).

Jesus thus gave his apostles a power greater than that of Israel's priests. The rabbis referred to this ancient priestly power in terms of "binding and loosing," and Jesus used those very words to describe what he was giving to his disciples. For the rabbis, to bind or loose meant to judge someone to be in communion with the chosen people—or cut off from its life and worship.

In bringing this old office to its fulfillment, Jesus added a new dimension. No longer would the authorities pass a sentence that was merely earthly. Since the Church shared the power of God incarnate, her power would extend as far as the power of God. "Truly, I say to you, whatever you bind on earth shall be bound in

heaven, and whatever you loose on earth shall be loosed in heaven"
(Mt 18:18). The Church could forgive sins in God's name. The
Church could lighten or waive the punishment that's due for sin.

All of that, however, presupposes a confession. Before the apostles could exercise their power over souls, they would need to hear
sins confessed aloud. Otherwise, they could not know what to bind
or loose.

The apostles exercised this authority and preached confession to
the first Christians. "If we confess our sins, [God] is faithful and
just," said St. John, "and will forgive our sins and cleanse us from
all unrighteousness" (1 Jn 1:9). St. Paul makes the further clarifi-
cation that "confession" is something you do "with your mouth,"
not just with your heart and mind (Rom 10:10). Paul considered
his mission to be a "ministry of reconciliation" (2 Cor 5:18)—
again, a role that had, in the Old Covenant, been carried out by the
Jerusalem priests, who brought about the forgiveness of sins
through the expiating sacrifices of the Temple.

St. James, for his part, took up the matter of confession at the
end of his discussion of the sacramental duties of the clergy. The
term he used for clergymen is the Greek *presbuterous*, which literally
means "elders," but which is the root of the English word *priest*.
Here's what James said: "Is any among you sick? Let him call for
the elders of the Church, and let them pray over him, anointing
him with oil in the name of the Lord; and the prayer of faith will
save the sick man, and the Lord will raise him up; and if he has
committed sins, he will be forgiven. Therefore confess your sins to
one another, and pray for one another, that you may be healed" (Jas
5:14–16).

James is clearly setting the practice of confession in connection
with the priest's healing ministry. Because priests are healers, we call

upon them to anoint our bodies when we are physically ill; and, *therefore*, even more eagerly, we go to them for the healing sacrament of forgiveness when our souls are sick with sin.

Note that St. James does not exhort his congregation to confess their sins to Jesus alone; nor does he tell them to confess their sins silently, in their hearts. They may do all these things, and all to their credit, but they will not yet be faithful to the word of God preached by St. James—not until they confess their sins aloud to "another," and specifically to a *presbyter*, a priest.

All of this was clear to the earliest churches. It is the teaching we find in the *Didache*, the most ancient Christian document we possess apart from the Scriptures. There we read: "Thou shalt confess thy transgressions in the Church and shalt not come unto prayer with an evil conscience." A later chapter speaks of the importance of confession before receiving Communion: "On the Lord's Day gather together, break bread, and give thanks [in Greek, *eucharistesate*], first confessing your sins so that your sacrifice may be pure."

Confession should always be individual, auricular—that is, spoken—and specific. The Church approves communal penance services but clearly states that they should lead the individual believer to an individual confession. Even if you receive general absolution on the battlefield, you're supposed to get yourself to a priest as soon as you can when the bullets stop flying.

Not long ago, it was customary for devout Catholics to go to confession every week. The lines on Saturday were very long. The saints have recommended that we go at least once a month.

Why has the practice dwindled in recent years, with some parishes offering the sacrament "by appointment only"? Recent popes have attributed this decline to a loss of the sense of sin. I think that's true. Ours is a no-fault culture. We have no-fault auto coverage and no-fault divorce. We've convinced ourselves that "I'm okay, you're okay," no matter what choices we make in life.

Yet the fact is that we're not okay, because we all sin, and we all *suffer* from our own sins and the sins of others. Thus, we're out of sync with the God who made us and we're out of sync with the world he made for us. Yes, God loves us just the way we are, but he loves us too much to keep us that way. We need to experience his forgiveness so that we can heal, and grow, and then practice forgiveness ourselves.

We need to recover a healthy sense of sin, so that we can recover spiritual health.

Ponder in Your Heart

It is better to confess one's sins than to harden one's heart.

—Pope St. Clement I, first century

17.

INDULGENCES

Imagine that you loaned a thousand dollars to a friend, who then came back to you and said, "You'll never guess what happened. I was at the mall, and I lost all the money, and I can't repay you for at least six months." There would be tension, no doubt, and perhaps a strained relationship.

Now imagine that a good friend shows up and says to you: "I prayed for your debtor . . . so please release the debt." If a thousand dollars means as much to your budget as it means to mine, you might laugh out loud. The proposal would offend your sense of justice, and rightly so.

Some people try to portray indulgences that way—as the forgiveness of debt in the spiritual realm. But an indulgence is *not* the forgiveness of a debt. It's the *payment* of the debt. It's as if someone showed up and paid you the thousand dollars on behalf of your friend.

That's what Christ empowers Mary and the saints to do for us, and that's what Christ empowers us to do for others, even those who have died and are now in purgatory.

When we gain an indulgence, the Church draws from the treasury of merits of Christ and the saints—a treasury that is infinite—and applies those merits to us, assuming we are in the state of grace (we have not sinned grievously) and have fulfilled other conditions (confession, communion, and prayers for the pope). An indulgence may be plenary, remitting all the punishment due our sins, or partial.

It's an idea that is as old as biblical religion, and it has always been a part of biblical religion. The ancient rabbis bear witness to it, as do the Church Fathers. Let's consider it as we find it in the Old Testament.

Abraham was a just man who lived by faith, and his faith was manifest in many deeds. God tested him repeatedly, and Abraham consistently responded with faithful obedience. In Genesis 22, he faced the ultimate test: God commanded him to sacrifice his beloved son, Isaac. Abraham demonstrated his willingness, and he went with Isaac to Mount Moriah. But God spared Isaac and rewarded Abraham with a promise of blessing to his descendants.

Yet his descendants forfeited that blessing in the most horrific way: by fashioning a bull-calf out of gold, and then worshipping it as an idol. It was a sin of catastrophic enormity, an act of senseless ingratitude toward the God who had, quite recently and quite miraculously, delivered Israel from slavery in Egypt. By committing such a sin, the Israelites merited death.

How did Moses deliver them from the punishment they deserved? By invoking the merit of their ancestors. He told the Lord: "Remember Abraham, Isaac, and Israel, your servants, to whom you swore by yourself, and said to them, 'I will multiply your descendants as the stars of heaven, and all this land that I have promised I will give to your descendants, and they shall inherit it for ever' " (Ex 32:13).

Moses did not try to plead the cause of the current generation, except insofar as they were offspring of the great patriarchs. In this story, we can see the temporal remission of punishment. God is going to destroy the Israelites; but he doesn't. We can see Moses' intercession, based upon the treasury of merits, the merit of the Fathers.

When the ancient rabbis discussed this story, they found no other way to explain it. The treasury of merit enabled them to safeguard God's mercy and his justice simultaneously. They applied the same principles to the stories of Noah, whose righteousness served to redeem future generations from the ravages of the flood, and David, whose goodness alone saved his son Solomon from the disaster he merited for himself.

The Church Fathers understood these Old Testament stories as but dim shadows of what God the Father now does through Christ. In the Old Covenant, the merit passed from Abraham to Isaac to Israel and then to all the descendants of Israel. Now, it moves from the Father through the Son in the Spirit to Mary, the saints, the martyrs, and all of us as well.

We live in communion with others. That's true in the natural order; it's also true in the supernatural order. The saints bear our burdens, and we too must "bear one another's burdens" (Gal 6:2). St. Paul understood how this worked, and he said: "in my flesh I complete what is lacking in Christ's afflictions for the sake of his body, that is, the Church" (Col 1:24).

On the cross, Jesus pronounced, "It is finished." The perfect work of our redemption was indeed accomplished. But in another sense it was only just beginning—because, at that moment, Christ gave forth his Spirit: he empowered us, through the Holy Spirit, to share in his own life, death, and resurrection. He transferred to us everything that he had merited. And so, at the end of his earthly pilgrimage, he could say, "It is finished," and entrust his redemptive work to the Holy Spirit. The Spirit applies to the saints—and to all of us—what Christ merited through his life, death, and resurrection.

All of this is an ordered economy. It is a "managed economy," because God gave the apostles and their successors, the pope and the bishops, the power of binding and loosing (Mt 16:19, 18:18). So today we see the Church exercising the authority that Moses once exercised on Mount Sinai, the right and the duty to call upon the merits of the saints.

The Church has distributed these merits by attaching them to certain prayers, works, and sacrifices that build up Christ's body. They range from giving up smoking for a day to undertaking a pilgrimage to the Holy Land.

When the Church speaks of indulgences, it speaks of them in the context of "the full enjoyment of the benefits of the family of God" (see below). So go ahead and indulge yourself. Indulge yourself for the sake of others as well—for the living and for the dead. We're free to do so because God is at once just, merciful, and indeed indulgent. He is our Father. And he has arranged everything so that even supernatural life is a family affair.

Ponder in Your Heart

There reigns among men, by the hidden and benign mystery of the divine will, a supernatural solidarity whereby the sin of one harms the others just as the holiness of one also benefits the others. Thus the Christian faithful give each other mutual aid to attain their supernatural aim. A testimony of this solidarity is manifested in Adam himself, whose sin is passed on through propagation to all men. But of this supernatural solidarity the greatest and most perfect principle, foundation and example is Christ himself to communion with whom God has called us . . .

Following in the footsteps of Christ, the Christian faithful have always endeavored to help one another on the path leading to the heavenly Father through prayer, the exchange of spiritual goods and penitential expiation. The more they have been immersed in the fervor of charity, the more they have imitated Christ in his sufferings, carrying their crosses in expiation for their own sins and those of others, certain that they could help their brothers to obtain salvation from God the Father of mercies. This is the very ancient dogma of the Communion of the Saints, whereby the life of each individual son of God in Christ and through Christ is joined by a wonderful link to the life of all his other Christian brothers in the supernatural unity of the Mystical Body of Christ till, as it were, a single mystical person is formed.

Thus is explained the "treasury of the Church" . . . the infinite and inexhaustible value the expiation and the merits of Christ Our Lord have before God, offered as they were so that all of mankind could be set free from sin and attain communion with the Father. It is Christ the Redeemer himself in whom the satisfactions and merits of his redemption exist and find their force. This treasury also includes the truly immense, unfathomable and ever pristine value before God of the prayers and good works of the Blessed Virgin Mary and all the saints, who following in the footsteps of Christ the Lord and by his grace have sanctified their lives and fulfilled the mission entrusted to them by the Father. Thus while attaining their own salvation, they have also cooperated in the salvation of their brothers in the unity of the Mystical Body.

"For all who are in Christ, having his spirit, form one Church and cleave together in him" (Eph 4:16) . . . For this reason there certainly exists between the faithful who have already reached their heavenly home, those who are expiating their sins in purgatory and those who are still pilgrims on earth a perennial link of charity and an abundant exchange of all the goods by which, with the expiation of all the sins of the entire Mystical Body, divine justice is placated. God's mercy is thus led to forgiveness, so that sincerely repentant sinners may participate as soon as possible in the full enjoyment of the benefits of the family of God.

—Pope Paul VI, twentieth century

18.

....

INTERCESSION OF THE SAINTS

The apostle Paul referred to himself as "the foremost of sinners" (1 Tim 1:15). But he knew also that he was a saint.

To St. Paul, as to all the Catholic Church, all Christians are "saints" by virtue of their baptism. "Saint" means "holy one," and Christians are made holy not by anything they've learned or done, but by the indwelling of almighty God. We are holy because we are temples of the Holy Spirit—and, in Paul's worldview, nothing on earth is holier than God's Temple.

Thus, St. Paul's Letter to the Colossians begins: "To the *saints* and faithful brethren in Christ at Colossae: We always thank God, the Father of our Lord Jesus Christ, when we pray for you, because we have heard of your faith in Christ Jesus and of the love which you have for all the *saints* . . . May you be strengthened with all power, according to his glorious might, for all endurance and patience with joy, giving thanks to the Father, who has qualified us to share in the inheritance of the *saints* in light" (Col 1:2–12; italics added).

Holiness—sainthood—is simply the common Christian vocation. But, in that short passage from Colossians, Paul also distinguished between the saints on earth (Col 1:2) and the "saints in light" (Col 1:12)—what Catholic devotion would later call, respectively, the "Church militant" and the "Church triumphant." The Epistle to the Hebrews (12:1) tells us that the latter are "a cloud of witnesses" around the former.

To the saints on earth who share our calling, we give our love. To the saints in light, we give a special honor called veneration. It's not the same kind of honor we give to God alone. It is more like the profound respect we owe our parents and grandparents. We love them so much that we frame their photos and give them a prominent place in our home. We shouldn't hesitate to ask our parents for prayer; nor should we hesitate to ask our ancestors in the faith.

St. Paul himself asked for the intercession of the "saints" in Colossae (see Col 4:3). For as we share in the life and divine nature of Jesus Christ, so we share in his singular office as the "one mediator between God and men" (1 Tim 2:5). So St. Paul could "urge that supplications, prayers, intercessions, and thanksgivings be made for all men" (1 Tim 2:1). He could, moreover, promise to assure the saints in Colossae of his own intercession on their behalf: "we have not ceased to pray for you" (Col 1:9).

Knowing what we know from elsewhere in the New Testament, we can be certain that St. Paul's intercession has not ceased, even today. The book of Revelation (6:9–10) shows the martyrs in heaven, very much aware of events on earth, and crying out to God for redress. Jesus himself, in one of his parables, depicts a heavenly intercession (Lk 16:27–28).

The early Christians kept a lively devotion to the Communion of Saints. It was not simply a matter of honoring their ancestors, because they did not think of the saints as dead and therefore removed from their presence. The saints were more present to the Church on earth, because the saints lived in the presence of God. The saints were not dead; indeed, they were more alive than the Church on earth.

The devotion of the early Christians is evident in hundreds of archaeological finds, in great artworks and in semi-literate graffiti, in monuments and on common household items. The cry of the Church on earth goes up constantly to the saints in heaven: "pray for us" and "bless us."

The saints in glory were part of the great family of the Church, the anniversaries of their deaths celebrated as "birthdays" by the Christians who outlived them, and many of them observed perpetually in the calendar of the universal Church.

The scholar Peter Brown has emphasized repeatedly that this was not the superstitious devotion of the "rabble." It was not a holdover from paganism. In fact, the pagans were horrified by Christian devotion to the saints, and they condemned it as unseemly!

No, it was the greatest Scripture scholars of ancient Christianity who kept the liveliest devotion to the saints. We find it spelled out most eloquently in the writings of those biblicists we now know as St. Jerome, St. Augustine, and St. John Chrysostom.

So great was Jerome's devotion that he used to spend his Sunday afternoons strolling among the martyrs' remains in the dark corridors of the Roman catacombs.

St. John Chrysostom, in the fourth century, marveled at the role reversals created by the cult of the saints. "Even the emperor . . . who wears the purple and sets everything shaking at his nod often throws himself face down upon the martyr's tomb and calls for that saint's prayers"—a saint who, in earthly life, might have been a commoner or of no-account! Who's shaking now? He spoke also of humble wives who implored the saints' protection for their husbands who had undertaken perilous journeys.

St. Augustine preached often about the lives of the saints, and he wrote several extended defenses of Catholic devotion to the saints. He was responding mostly to attacks from the Manicheans—heretics who were so flaky that they were really more pagan than Christian. Yet their arguments are strikingly similar to those we hear from anti-Catholics today. "The prayers of the martyrs help us," he preached. "Indeed, it is through these solemnities that *your* [italics added] sanctity is commemorated . . . lest we think that we are giving something to the martyrs when we celebrate their most solemn days. They do not need our festivals. For they rejoice in heaven with the angels. They rejoice with us not so much if we honor them as if we imitate them."

Again, I hear echoes of St. Paul, who said, "Be imitators of me as I am of Christ" (I Cor 1:11). To venerate St. Paul is to glorify Christ for his grace made manifest in the life of his family on earth. St. Paul said: "It is no longer I who live, but Christ who lives in me" (Gal 2:20). Christ indeed lives in all the saints, and he makes them even more perfectly themselves.

It is a deep fellow feeling, a family feeling, that Christians share with the saints. The fourth-century bishop St. Paulinus of Nola placed himself under the patronage of St. Felix, a martyr. In a poem he addressed the saint as "revered father, everlasting patron, Felix my nurse, Felix, dear friend of Christ."

In all the history of Christianity, so little has changed. We hear the same terms today addressed to beloved saints from down the ages: St. Jude Thaddeus, St. Francis of Assisi, St. Anthony of

Padua, St. Catherine Laboure, St. Thérèse of Lisieux, St. Maximilian Kolbe, Padre Pio.

To such figures we do not hesitate to say, "Pray for us!"

Ponder in Your Heart

It is true that Christians pay religious honor to the memory of the martyrs, both to excite us to imitate them and to gain a share in their merits and the assistance of their prayers. Yet we do not build altars to any martyr, but to the God of martyrs, although it is to the *memory* of the martyrs. No one presiding at the altar in the saints' burial place ever says, "We bring an offering to you, O Peter!" or "O Paul!" or "O Cyprian!" The offering is made to God, who gave the crown of martyrdom, while it is *in memory* [italics added] of those thus crowned.

The emotion is increased by the associations of the place, and love is excited both toward those who are our examples, and toward him by whose help we may follow such examples. We regard the martyrs with the same affectionate intimacy that we feel towards holy men of God in this life, when we know that their hearts are prepared to endure the same suffering for the truth of the Gospel. There is more devotion in our feeling toward the martyrs, because we know that their conflict is over; and we can speak with greater confidence in praise of those already victors in heaven, than of those still combating here.

What is properly divine worship, the Greeks call *latria* (for which there is no word in Latin), and both in doctrine and in practice we give this only to God. To this [divine] worship belongs the offering of sacrifices, as we see in the word *idolatry*, which means the giving of this worship to idols. Accordingly we never offer, or require anyone to offer, sacrifice to a martyr, or to a holy soul, or to any angel. Anyone falling into this error is instructed by doctrine, either in the way of correction or of caution. For holy beings themselves, whether saints or angels, refuse to accept what they know to be due to God alone. We see this in Paul and Barnabas, when the men of Lycaonia wished to sacrifice to them as gods, on account of the miracles they performed. They rent their clothes, and restrained the people, crying out to them, and persuading them that they were not gods. We see it also in the angels, as we read in the Apocalypse that an angel would not allow himself to be worshipped, and said to his worshipper, "I am your fellow-servant, and of your brethen" (Rev 19:10).

—St. Augustine of Hippo, fourth century

VI

Love of My Life

19.

THE ROSARY

"For behold, henceforth all generations will call me blessed" (Lk 1:48).

Every time we pray the Rosary, we fulfill that prophecy at least fifty times. We call the Virgin Mary "blessed," using the inspired words of Holy Writ. We address her with the greeting of the angel Gabriel: "Hail, full of grace, the Lord is with you" (Lk 1:28). We proclaim her privileges, using the words of Elizabeth her kins-woman: "Blessed are you among women, and blessed is the fruit of your womb!" (Lk 1:42). To repeat these words is a delight, because they're rich with meaning, amplified by the Gospel scenes that are the focus of our meditations.

The Rosary is a time-proven method of meditative prayer. For centuries the popes have recommended it, the saints have prayed it daily. It is beloved by laborers, by children, by busy commuters, and by scientific geniuses. It was the favorite prayer of the great biolo-gist Louis Pasteur.

Praying the Rosary, we repeat certain prayers as we ponder certain events ("mysteries") in the lives of Jesus and Mary, and we count our repetitions using beads strung together in groups of ten. Yet, like so many other devotions, the Rosary is a form that allows for variation. The Rosary of the "Seven Sorrows," for example, includes seven groups of seven beads. Some people end their Rosary with a "Hail, Holy Queen," others with the Litany of Loreto, and still others with a series of prayers for the pope. Some even conclude their Marian marathon with all of the above! There are ethnic varieties as well: pious Germans, for instance, have the custom of improvising a mystery-specific insertion for each Hail Mary. For example, while meditating on the Annunciation, they pray, "Blessed is the fruit of your womb, Jesus . . . the Word who became flesh." While meditating on the Crucifixion, they might pray, "Blessed is the fruit of your womb, Jesus . . . who died for our sins."

The Church has officially recognized twenty "mysteries" appropriate for meditation. We should find them all in Scripture, in order to meditate on them more fruitfully: the five Joyful Mysteries (the Annunciation, the Visitation, the Nativity, the Presentation, and the Finding in the Temple); the five Luminous Mysteries (the Baptism of Our Lord, the Wedding Feast at Cana, the Proclamation of the Kingdom, the Transfiguration, and the Institution of the Eucharist at the Last Supper); the five Sorrowful Mysteries (the Agony in the Garden, the Scourging, the Crowning with Thorns, the Carrying of the Cross, and the Crucifixion); and the five Glorious Mysteries (the Resurrection, the Ascension, the Descent of the Holy Spirit, the Assumption, and the Coronation of Our Lady). Pope John Paul II suggested that each set of mysteries be assigned to certain days of the week: Joyful on Mondays and Saturdays, Luminous on Thursdays, Sorrowful on Tuesdays and Fridays,

Glorious on Wednesdays and Sundays. There are other, "unofficial" sets of mysteries in circulation, too, the products of occasional groundswells of scriptural and Marian piety. Through the years I've seen many—the Eucharistic Mysteries, for example, the Healing Mysteries, and the Mysteries of the Church. I never saw a set I didn't like, though for my own prayer I'm partial to the basic twenty.

The Rosary *works,* on a human level, because it engages the whole person. It involves our speech and our hearing. It occupies our mind and incites our emotions. It assigns a task to our fingertips, those sensitive organs of touch. If we pray before a sacred image, we feed our meditation through yet another bodily sense. This is how the risen Lord confirms the faith of his disciples: "See my hands and my feet, that it is I myself; handle me, and see" (Lk 24:39). It is not enough for us merely to hear him—never mind only read his words. We want him to fill up our senses.

And he does, thanks to the love of his mother. In the Scriptures, she appears as the first disciple. When gentiles come from far away in search of Jesus, they find "the child with Mary his mother" (Mt 2:11). When she sees people in need, she intercedes for them (Jn 2:3). When Jesus dies on the cross, abandoned by his friends, she remains with him; and Jesus gives her to his "beloved disciple" (that means you and me), saying, "Behold, your mother" (Jn 19:27). Thus, she helps us to meditate in a way that she uniquely can. She helps us as his mother—and so, an eyewitness of his whole life. But she helps us also as our mother, given to us by Jesus, loving us as only a mother can.

With Mary we watch the events of our salvation as they unfold. We give ourselves to the Rosary as a multisensory experience. People get hung up when they try too hard to master the various elements as individual tasks: saying the prayers, fingering the beads, and thinking very hard about the Gospel scenes with excruciatingly exact historical verisimilitude.

No. The Rosary works best when we stop working—when we stop multitasking and abandon ourselves like children to the time we're spending with our mother. The best way to get ourselves to relax is by praying the Rosary itself! In the years just before his election as Pope Benedict XVI, Cardinal Joseph Ratzinger told an interviewer: "repetition is a way of settling oneself into the rhythm of tranquility. It's not so much a matter of consciously concentrating on the meaning of each single word, but allowing myself on the contrary to be carried away by the calm of repetition and of steady rhythm. So much the more so, since this text does not lack content. It brings great images and visions and above all the figure of Mary—and then, through her, the figure of Jesus—before my eyes and in my soul."

There is nothing vain about such repetition. To pray in this way is to please Our Lord, who told his disciples, "And in praying do not heap up empty phrases as the Gentiles do" (Mt 6:7). True Christians, on the contrary, never tire of repeating the Rosary's prayers, which are phrases of fulfillment.

The best place to pray the Rosary is with the family. When Father Patrick Peyton said, "The family that prays together stays together," he was talking about the Rosary. Pope John Paul II was a tireless promoter of the family Rosary, and even coined a title for the Blessed Virgin, "Queen of the Family," which he attached to the end of the most popular Marian litany. All these initiatives surely pleased Our Lady. After Mother Teresa of Calcutta endured a harrowing vision of Calvary, she recorded that Mary reassured her: "Fear not. Teach them to say the Rosary—the family Rosary—and all will be well."

It is difficult to make the family Rosary fit the schedule of a busy household. There was a time in my family when we found it almost impossible to trap all our sports-minded teenagers in the house at once. So we did what we could. We locked onto the one time when we were almost always together—dinner—and we concluded our meal with a decade. This served as our "down payment" on the family Rosary till we could do a better job of taming our schedules.

Though the family Rosary is a powerful grace, the experience of the Rosary is a very individual thing. People differ in their capacity for certain prayers, as we differ in everything else. It's true even of popes. Pope John Paul II was known to pray many decades of the Rosary every day. Pope Benedict has confessed that sometimes the intensity of three decades of meditation is overwhelming, and he has to pause the devotion.

Not all of us will experience the Rosary with such emotion. Some of us have a hard enough time keeping focus—even with all our senses engaged.

Nevertheless, it would be sinful pride to abandon such a prayer simply because we don't pray it well. When my children were very small, they would often present me with "artworks" that were really no more than smudges and scribbles. But to me they were masterpieces—and more: they were sacraments of love. My life would have been impoverished if any of my children had abandoned the practice because, at age four, they could not paint the *Mona Lisa*.

To God and to the Blessed Virgin, all our efforts at prayer are precious. When we persevere in praying the Rosary, we become like little children (see Mt 18:3), children of Mary, children of our heavenly Father.

Blessed Pope John XXIII, a childlike son of Mary, had excellent advice for those who grew frustrated with their own inattention as they tried to pray the Rosary. Such people gave up, with the excuse that they'd rather pray no Rosary than a bad one. He corrected them, saying that a "bad Rosary" is one left unsaid.

Ponder in Your Heart

The Rosary, though clearly Marian in character, is at heart a Christocentric prayer. In the sobriety of its elements, it has *all the depth of the Gospel message in its entirety*, of which it can be said to be a compendium. It is an echo of the prayer of Mary, her perennial *Magnificat* for the work of the redemptive incarnation which began in her virginal womb. With the Rosary, the Christian people *sits at the school of Mary* and is led to contemplate the beauty on the face of Christ and to experience the depths of his love. Through the Rosary the faithful receive abundant grace, as though from the very hands of the mother of the Redeemer.

—Pope John Paul II, twentieth century

20.

SCAPULARS AND MEDALS

Medals have been part of Catholic life since the early centuries of the Church. Archaeologists have turned up countless examples of such personal ornaments, the most popular being the cross. Some are free-standing, some are inscribed on a medallion. Medals of the Blessed Virgin Mary have always been popular, and museums have examples dating back to antiquity. The saints, too, have adorned the bodies of believers since way back. The early Church in Egypt was especially devoted to St. Menas, whose grave was at a spring renowned for its healing waters. St. Menas's image has turned up on pilgrim tokens as far away as France!

Through the centuries, the faithful have worn their devotion to many more saints. Browse the displays of any Catholic religious-goods store, and you can sometimes tell the saints' popularity by the number of medals that bear their likeness. Some are constants: St. Joseph, St. Jude, St. Benedict, St. Christopher, St. Thérèse, Padre Pio.

We wear scapulars, too. Scapulars are cloth items usually worn over the shoulders; and, like medals, they come in many varieties. So many, in fact, that we could write a book exclusively about scapulars and medals. Instead, however, I'd like to consider, in an exemplary way, the one I wear—the brown scapular of Our Lady—since it is, by far, the most commonly worn. And, besides, it's the one I've thought about the most!

A scapular is a sign of a commitment to the contemplative life. It originated as part of a monk's habit—the distinctive clothing he wears that sets him apart from other people. The scapular was, in the ancient world, a large overgarment that protected the monk's tunic while he was working. It was usually made of wool, and it was meant to stretch across the shoulders and down the front of the tunic, so that it looked almost cruciform. The word scapular comes from the Latin word for shoulder, *scapula*. Over time, the *scapular* became the most distinctive and characteristic form of a monk's clothing.

Over time, too, laypeople sought ways to share in the benefits of monastic life. We may not live cloistered behind monastery walls, but we long to be contemplatives in the middle of the world. So we take certain practices of prayer and meditation, and we modify them to our workaday lives. Some people pray the monastic "hours" of prayer, for example.

The small scapular is a sign of our share in the consecrated lives of monks and nuns. It's not as large as a full scapular. Specifically, the brown scapular is the way I share in the merits and good works of the Carmelite order.

The brown scapular consists of two small squares of brown cloth, one worn on the chest and the other on the back, joined by two strings or ribbons. When I decided to wear a scapular, I asked a priest to bless the item and "invest" me with it, using prayers that are approved for that purpose. In investing me with the scapular,

Father enrolled me in the Carmelite order (though the wearing of a scapular requires no vows, personal consecration, or lifetime commitments). Any priest or deacon may perform this ceremony.

From the start I was aware of the deep biblical roots of this practice. The Carmelite order traces its origins back to the Old Testament prophets Elijah and Elisha, who lived reclusive lives on remote Mount Carmel, in the hill country of Samaria (see 1 Kgs 18:19 and 2 Kgs 2:25, 4:25). The brown scapular itself evokes the "mantle of Elijah" that Elisha took up and wore as his own (see 2 Kgs 12:14).

The last of the prophets, St. John the Baptist, also wore poor and distinctive clothing—coarse garments made of camel hair (Mt 3:4)—and he lived as a desert recluse. He went, therefore, in the "spirit and power of Elijah" (Lk 1:17), and Jesus explicitly identified John with Elijah (Mk 9:13).

Christians of old read those Scriptures and longed to live like the prophets. Some discerned the call to make pilgrimage to the Holy Land and live as hermits on Mount Carmel. That was the beginning of the Carmelite order.

My share in that life is not so exotic or heroic. In fact, it's hidden—hidden in the traffic I merge with on the highway, hidden in the office I inhabit for hours every day, hidden amid the children who gather around my table every evening. It's hidden like the brown scapular I wear beneath my shirt. But it's no less real. My scapular reminds me, in all those circumstances, that I am joined with a *spiritual family* with members dispersed throughout the earth and throughout the centuries—a family whose members share certain ideals and customs.

The Carmelite order has always cultivated a particular and intense devotion to the Blessed Virgin Mary, and it is her image that usually appears on the brown scapular. It's said that, in the thirteenth century, she appeared to a Carmelite named St. Simon Stock (so named because he lived in the trunk of a tree!), and she told him that those who died "clothed in this habit will never suffer eternal fire."

Pope John Paul II said that the scapular is powerful precisely because it is a "habit" in every sense of the word, both a uniform and a pattern of good belief and good behavior. If we are faithful to the wearing of the scapular, we will be faithful to the life of Carmel—of Elijah and Elisha and John, of Jesus and Mary.

When I put the scapular back on every day, after I step out of the shower, I am deliberately taking on a life, refreshing my will to live a lifestyle that's heavenly even now. How could it fail to lead me to heaven in the end? It's no wonder that so many people kiss the scapular as they don it every day.

St. Thérèse of Lisieux said: "How happy I am that you are clothed in the holy scapular! It is a sure sign of predestination, and besides are you not more intimately united by means of it to your little sisters in Carmel?"

Again, there are many scapulars beside the brown scapular. The Benedictines have custody of one, the Dominicans another, the Norbertines still another. Since 1910, Catholics have been permitted to wear a scapular medal in place of a cloth scapular, and many people do. The scapular medal bears the image of Jesus' Sacred Heart on one side, and the image of Mary on the other.

Ponder in Your Heart

The sign of the scapular points to an effective synthesis of Marian spirituality, which nourishes the devotion of believers and makes them sensitive to the Virgin

Mother's loving presence in their lives. The scapular is essentially a "habit." Those who receive it are associated more or less closely with the Order of Carmel and dedicate themselves to the service of Our Lady for the good of the whole Church. Those who wear the scapular are thus brought into the land of Carmel, so that they may "eat its fruits and its good things" (cf. Jer 2:7), and experience the loving and motherly presence of Mary in their daily commitment to be clothed in Jesus Christ and to manifest him in their life for the good of the Church and the whole of humanity.

Therefore two truths are evoked by the sign of the scapular: on the one hand, the constant protection of the Blessed Virgin, not only on life's journey, but also at the moment of passing into the fullness of eternal glory; on the other, the awareness that devotion to her cannot be limited to prayers and tributes in her honor on certain occasions, but must become a "habit," that is, a permanent orientation of one's own Christian conduct, woven of prayer and interior life, through frequent reception of the sacraments and the concrete practice of the spiritual and corporal works of mercy. In this way the scapular becomes a sign of the "covenant" and reciprocal communion between Mary and the faithful: indeed, it concretely translates the gift of his mother, which Jesus gave on the cross to John and, through him, to all of us, and the entrustment of the beloved Apostle and of us to her, who became our spiritual Mother.

—Pope John Paul II, twentieth century

Epilogue

Jesus said to his disciples: "Ask, and it will be given you; seek, and you will find; knock, and it will be opened to you" (Mt 7:7).

Ask, seek, knock. We may be sure that he was not merely running down a list of quaint metaphors for prayer. More likely he was describing what everyone would recognize as the itinerary for a pilgrimage to the holy city. Pilgrims begin by asking the way. They travel in search of their destination: they seek. And they arrive as they knock at the city gates.

The way of Christian prayer is the way of a pilgrim. It is in the Sermon on the Mount that Jesus makes this connection. Jesus gives his teaching on pilgrimage immediately after he spells out his guidelines for the disciplines of prayer, fasting, and almsgiving (see Mt 6). From these words, all Catholic devotion has come forth, in all its richness and diversity. We have not yet begun to exhaust the possibilities for expressing our love, praise, thanksgiving, longing, wonder, and contrition.

Jesus left us with something to do. He left us not simply with a ready-made, gift-wrapped salvation, with all our questions answered and all our suffering ceased. Instead, he bid us to follow him along a road—a narrow road, to a narrow gate—in a great adventure. His road leads us to glory, but only by way of Calvary. We don't really know what awaits us around the next bend in the road; but we know that God is with us and he will answer us when we ask, seek, and knock—as we pray in the old accustomed ways.

All our lives, we are on pilgrimage. I began this book with the story of my late-night journey to the cross, my late-night Rosary on my neighborhood streets. I've come to learn, however, that my identity as a wayfarer is not occasional, but semi-permanent. For no longer do we journey to an earthly city, as Jesus' disciples did in the first century. Our Jerusalem is above, and we'll be asking, seeking, knocking till we're there. No longer do we seek an earthly temple; for God is building us up, by means of our prayer, as a heavenly temple.

So this book ends as it began. Beloved, we are God's children now, but we're not home yet. God is our Father, but he's in heaven. That's why we face crises, to remind us that we're pilgrims, still on the way. The Father uses these moments to change us, to speed us along the way, to transform pilgrims into saints.

We ask, seek, knock. We go our pilgrim way. We find the grace we need—though not always the grace we'd wish for, or the grace we'd expect. We receive the grace a perfect Father would give to his children who are on their way home.

Notes

Introduction

11. **Pope St. Leo the Great said:** St. Leo the Great, Sermon 74.2; see also *Catechism of the Catholic Church* (hereafter CCC), n. 1115.

11. **Pope Benedict XVI once said:** *Sacramentum Caritas* 64.

12. **"There are many things":** St. Gregory of Nyssa, *On the Baptism of Christ,* in Scott Hahn and Mike Aquilina, *Living the Mysteries* (Huntington, IN: Our Sunday Visitor, 2003), 44.

Chapter 1: Holy Water

21. **At the end of the second century:** Tertullian, *On Prayer* 13.

22. **St. Thomas Aquinas taught:** For a fuller discussion of St. Thomas's method, see my essay "Search the Scriptures: Reading the Old Testament with Jesus, John and Thomas Aquinas," in *Scripture Matters: Essays on Reading the Bible from the Heart of the Church* (Steubenville, OH: Emmaus Road, 2003).

22. **With Jesus, however:** St. Thomas Aquinas, *Commentary on St. John* 443.

23. **According to St. Thomas:** Ibid., 577.

23. **St. Teresa of Avila wrote:** St. Teresa of Avila, *The Book of Her Life* 31.4, in *Saint Teresa of Avila: Collected Works,* trans. Kieran Kavanaugh, vol. I, (Washington, D.C.: ICS, 1987), 265.

24. **King and Lord of all things:** Adapted from the Wobbermin translation, *Bishop Sarapion's Prayer-Book* (London: SPCK, 1899), 68–69.

Chapter 2: The Sign of the Cross

25. **Cardinal Joseph Ratzinger (the future Pope Benedict XVI):** Joseph Cardinal Ratzinger, *The Spirit of the Liturgy* (San Francisco: Ignatius, 2000), 177.

26. **At the end of the second century:** Tertullian, *The Chaplet* 3.

26. **Tertullian praised his wife:** Tertullian, *To His Wife* 2.5.

27. **We raise the hand first:** St. Francis de Sales, *The Standard of the Cross* 3.I, quoted in Nicholas Gihr, *The Holy Sacrifice of the Mass* (St. Louis: Herder, 1939), 349-350. Language modernized slightly.

27. **The cross is an image:** For a fuller treatment of the relationship between the Trinity and the cross, see my book *First Comes Love: Finding Your Family in the Church and the Trinity,* 2nd ed. (New York: Doubleday, 2002).

28. **In his groundbreaking work:** St. Basil the Great, *On the Holy Spirit* 27.66.

29. **It is, in the words of Cardinal Ratzinger:** Ratzinger, *The Spirit of the Liturgy,* 178.

29. **"Making the sign of the Cross":** Pope Benedict XVI, Angelus address, September II, 2005.

29. **When we cross ourselves:** Romano Guardini, *Sacred Signs* (St. Louis: Pio Decimo, 1956), 13–14.

Chapter 3: Baptism

30. **Life begins at baptism:** For a fuller treatment of baptism, see my book *Swear to God: The Promise and Power of the Sacraments* (New York: Doubleday, 2004).

33. **Yet baptism, he said:** St. Ambrose of Milan, Letter 72 (to Constantius), par. 16.

34. **"We are Christians because of a covenant":** Romano Guardini, *Meditations Before Mass* (Manchester, NH: Sophia Institute Press, 1993), 191.

35. **In considering . . . the gift:** Pope John Paul II, apostolic exhortation *Christifideles Laici* (On the Vocation and Mission of the Lay Faithful in the Church and in the World), nn. 11 and 17, December 30, 1988.

Chapter 4: The Mass

37. **Long before the New Testament books:** I have explored the Mass in many books, among them *The Lamb's Supper: The Mass as Heaven on Earth* (New York: Doubleday, 1999); *Swear to God: The Promise and Power of the Sacraments* (New York: Doubleday, 2004); *Letter and Spirit: From Written Text to Living Word in the Liturgy* (New York: Doubleday, 2005); and *Catholic for a Reason III: Scripture and the Mystery of the Mass* (Steubenville, OH: Emmaus Road, 2004).

38. **Many years before he became pope:** See his discussion in *Behold the Pierced One* (San Francisco: Ignatius, 1986), 83–85.

41. **Here we must apply our minds:** St. John Chrysostom, Homily 14 on Hebrews, n. 3.

Chapter 5: Guardian Angels

47. **Let us look for a moment:** St. Josemaría Escrivá, *Christ Is Passing By* (Princeton, NJ: Scepter, no date), 139–141.

Chapter 6: Advent and Christmas

55. **Advent is celebrated for four weeks:** Jacobus de Voragine, *The Golden Legend* (London: Longmans, Green, 1941), 2-3 (language modernized slightly).

Chapter 7: Confirmation

59. **To be saved means nothing less:** I discuss Confirmation, with the other sacraments, in my book *Swear to God.*

61. **The Church teaches that confirmation:** See CCC, n. 1304.

62. **Now that you have been "baptized into Christ":** St. Cyril of Jerusalem, *Mystagogical Sermons* 3.1–3, in Edward Yarnold, *The Awe-Inspiring Rites of Initiation* (Collegeville, MN: Liturgical Press, 1994), 81–83.

Chapter 8: Marriage

64. **In John's apocalypse:** I discuss marriage at greater length in my books *Swear to God, First Comes Love,* and *Catholic for a Reason IV: Scripture and the Mystery of Marriage and Family Life* (Steubenville, OH: Emmaus Road, 2007).

65. **Jon Levenson, a contemporary Jewish scholar:** Jon Levenson, *Sinai and Zion: An Entry into the Jewish Bible* (San Francisco: HarperCollins, 1985), 76.

65. **He goes on to explain:** Ibid., 77.

65. **Levenson concludes:** Ibid., 79.

65. **Rabbi Michael Fishbane traces:** Michael Fishbane, *JPS Bible Commentary: Haftarot* (Philadelphia: Jewish Publication Society, 2002), 555–556.

69. **"Every celebration," Augustine said:** Quoted in Claude Chavasse, *The Bride of Christ* (London: Faber and Faber, 1939), 147.

70. **Marriage has God for its Author:** Pope Leo XIII, encyclical letter *Arcanum Divinae,* n. 19, February 10, 1880.

Chapter 9: Priesthood

71. **After years of researching and praying:** I discuss Holy Orders in my books *Swear to God* and *Scripture Matters.*

75. **St. Augustine looked the same way:** St. Augustine, *Reflections on the Psalms* 44.32, quoted in Henri de Lubac, *The Motherhood of the Church* (San Francisco: Ignatius Press, 1982), 90.

76. **The reason that God-loving men of old:** Eusebius of Caesarea, *Demonstration of the Gospel* 1.9, quoted in Stefan Heid, *Celibacy in the Early Church* (San Francisco: Ignatius Press, 2000), 119.

Chapter 10: Anointing of the Sick

78. **This is the sacrament we know:** I discuss this, with the other sacraments, at greater length in my book *Swear to God.*

80. **The Old and the New Testament:** Aimé Georges Martimort, *The Signs of the New Covenant* (Collegeville, MN: Liturgical Press, 1963), 264–265, 268.

Chapter 11: Incense

87. **A Jewish theologian of the first century:** Philo of Alexandria, *The Special Laws* 1.171.

88. **Sovereign Lord Jesus Christ:** *Liturgy of St. James,* adapted from vol. 7 of *Ante-Nicene Fathers* (1994; repr., Peabody, MA: Hendrickson, 2004), 537, 540, 549.

Chapter 12: Candles

90. **In his commentary on Leviticus:** Levine, *Leviticus,* 217.

92. **The greatest Scripture scholar:** St. Jerome, *Against Vigilantius* 7.

92. **Jerome recalls the funeral:** St. Jerome, *Letters* 108.

92. **numberous wicks:** St. Jerome, *Against Vigilantius* 7.

92. **St. Paulinus of Nola described:** St. Paulinus of Nola, *Carmen* 111.

93. **The lamps that you kindle:** St. Gregory Nazianzen, *Oration* 40.46.

Chapter 13: Sacred Images

96. **The most eloquent of the iconodules:** St. Theodore of Studion, quoted in Christoph Schonborn, *God's Human Face* (San Francisco: Ignatius, 1994), 234.

97. **Since some find fault:** St. John of Damascus, *Exposition of the Orthodox Faith* 4.16.

Chapter 14: Relics

102. **The emperor Julian:** Julian the Apostate, quoted in Peter Brown, *The Cult of the Saints: Its Rise and Function in Latin Christianity* (Chicago: University of Chicago Press, 1982), 7.

103. **Addressed to a heretic:** St. Jerome, *Against Vigilantius* 5.

Chapter 15: Fasting and Mortification

108. **Let us fall to fasting:** St. Thomas More, quoted in E. E. Reynolds, ed., *The Heart of Thomas More* (London: Burns and Oates, 1966), 170–171.

Chapter 16: Confession

113. **Confession is the way:** My book-length study of confession is *Lord, Have Mercy: The Healing Power of Confession* (New York: Doubleday, 2003).

117. **the teaching we find in the *Didache*:** *Didache* 4.14.

117. **A later chapter speaks:** Ibid. 14.1.

118. **It is better to confess:** St. Clement of Rome, *To the Corinthians* 51.

Chapter 17: Indulgences

122. **There reigns among men:** Pope Paul VI, apostolic constitution *Indulgentiarum Doctrina*, chap. 2, January 1, 1967.

Chapter 18: Intercession of the Saints

127. **St. John Chrysostom, in the fourth century:** St. John Chrysostom, "On All the Martyrs," in *The Cult of the Saints* (Crestwood, NY: St. Vladimir Seminary Press, 2006), 247.

128. **St. Augustine preached often:** St. Augustine, *Sermons* 325.1.

128. **The fourth-century bishop St. Paulinus:** St. Paulinus of Nola, *Carmina* 21.

129. **To such figures we do not hesitate:** I discuss the Communion of Saints at greater length in my book *Reasons to Believe: How to Understand, Explain, and Defend the Catholic Faith* (New York: Doubleday, 2007).

129. **It is true that Christians:** St. Augustine, *Reply to Faustus* 20.21; see also *City of God* 8.27.

Chapter 19: The Rosary

133. **We call the Virgin Mary "blessed":** For a fuller discussion of the Church's Marian doctrine and piety, see my books *Hail, Holy Queen* and *Catholic for a Reason II.*

136. **In the years just before his election:** Joseph Cardinal Ratzinger, *God and the World* (San Francisco: Ignatius, 2002), 319.

136. **Mother Teresa of Calcutta endured a harrowing vision:** Mother Teresa, *Come Be My Light* (New York: Doubleday, 2007), 99.

138. **The Rosary, though clearly Marian:** Pope John Paul II, apostolic letter *Rosarium Mariae Virginis,* n. 1, October 16, 2002 (italics in original).

Chapter 20: Scapulars and Medals

140. **The word *scapular* comes from:** For the earliest history of the scapular, see Elizabeth Kuhns, *The Habit: A History of the Clothing of Catholic Nuns* (New York: Doubleday, 2003), 67–69.

142. **St. Thérèse of Lisieux said:** St. Thérèse of Lisieux, letter to her sister Celine, in *Letters of St. Thérèse of Lisieux*, vol. 2 (Washington: ICS Publications, 1982), 866.

142. **The sign of the Scapular points:** Pope John Paul II, *Message to the Carmelite Family*, n. 5, March 25, 2001.